D0900199

Colonial Settlements in America

Jamestown
New Amsterdam
Philadelphia
Plymouth
St. Augustine
Santa Fe
Williamsburg
Yerba Buena

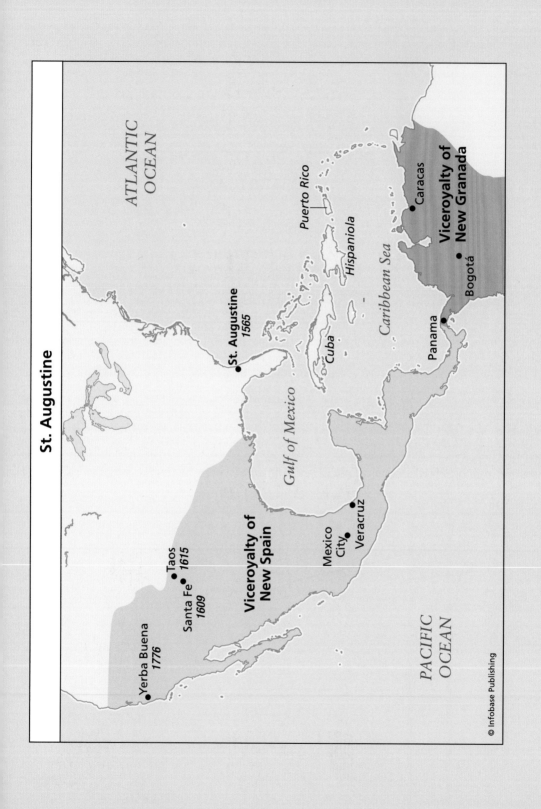

Colonial Settlements in America

St. Augustine

Shane Mountjoy

SERIES EDITOR

Tim McNeese

CHELSEA HOUSE
PUBLISHERS

An imprint of Infobase Publishing

Frontis: The Spanish town of St. Augustine was established in 1565 and is the oldest continuously occupied European-founded settlement in what is today the United States.

St. Augustine

Copyright © 2007 by Infobase Publishing

Chelsea House
An imprint of Infobase Publishing
132 West 31st Street
New York, NY 10001

ISBN-10: 0-7910-9337-9   ISBN-13: 978-0-7910-9337-5

Library of Congress Cataloging-in-Publication Data
Mountjoy, Shane, 1967-
  St. Augustine / Shane Mountjoy.
    p. cm. — (Colonial settlements in America)
  Includes bibliographical references and index.
  Audience: Grades 7-8.
  ISBN 0-7910-9337-9 (hardcover)
  1. Saint Augustine (Fla.)—History—Juvenile literature. 2. Spaniards—Florida—Saint Augustine—History—Juvenile literature. 3. Florida—History—To 1821—Juvenile literature. I. Title. II. Title: Saint Augustine. III. Series.
  F319.S2M68 2007
  975.9'18—dc22   2006028364

Series design by Erika K. Arroyo
Cover design by Ben Peterson

Printed in the United States of America

Bang EJB 10 9 8 7 6 5 4 3 2 1

This book is printed on acid-free paper.

Contents

1

A Line in the Sand

Pedro Menéndez de Avilés, the Spanish governor of Florida, stood on the beach looking east, toward the rising sun. The morning sun cast down its warm rays in the cool air of a late September day in 1565. The warm waters of the Atlantic Ocean gently lapped against the sand in an endless series of waves. Menéndez sighed deeply, then drew in a deep breath of fresh sea air.

The governor looked across the small bay. Late the night before, he and 50 of his men had arrived at the south end of Anastasia Island. There they quietly made camp for the night. Although it was dark, the Spaniards had seen the many campfires of the French force. The governor wanted to get a better idea of how many were in the other camp, so he climbed a tree for a better view.

Menéndez knew that the opposing force was sure to be much larger than his own. Fortunately, an inlet of water that fed into the Atlantic Ocean separated the two groups. More importantly, Menéndez knew that the French force were the survivors

PEDRO MENENDEZ DE AVILES.
Natural de Avilés en Asturias, Comendador
de la orden de Santiago, Conquistador de la Florida, nombrado Grāl. de la Armada contra Inglaterra.
Murió en Santander N.º 1574. á los 55. de edad

In August 1565, Pedro Menéndez de Avilés founded the first permanent settlement in what later would become the United States. Avilés named the town in honor of St. Augustine of Hippo, whose feast day is celebrated on August 28, the day the Spanish first spotted the Florida coastline.

of a shipwreck. He also knew that, just days earlier, these men were on one of the ships that had threatened the new Spanish fort of St. Augustine. The winds of an approaching hurricane had pushed the ships away from the fort. Local Native Americans came to the fort and told Menéndez that one of the ships had sunk. Now, the survivors from that ship were making their way north along the shoreline, toward St. Augustine.

From where he stood, the governor could see more and more of the French soldiers on the opposite shore. The men looked hungry. They walked along the shore, looking for anything they might eat. With his dark eyes, Menéndez watched them carefully and considered the situation. In this place, all seemed at peace, all seemed calm. But within the heart and mind of Menéndez, all was anything but peaceful or calm. The governor weighed his options. He knew what must be done, but the right choice seemed wrong. His decision would forever make him a villain in history.

Menéndez faced a difficult choice. The French soldiers across the inlet were his sworn enemies. Just days earlier, these same men had tried to attack the fledgling settlement at St. Augustine. Only a timely hurricane saved the young colony from destruction. The storm blew the French ships south of St. Augustine onto the jagged reefs. All four French ships sank. The men across the bay were all survivors from the ship that had been separated from the other three. The Spanish leader knew that the French could have easily destroyed his force, and probably would have were it not for the weather.

In order to gather more information, Menéndez had already changed his clothes. No longer did he wear the uniform of an officer. Instead, he wore those of any ordinary sailor. Thus, when he appeared on the shore opposite the French survivors, Pedro Menéndez appeared to be no one of consequence. But looks can be deceiving: Pedro Menéndez was anything but ordinary. The French soldiers would soon discover this for themselves.

The governor stood in plain sight, hoping the French soldiers might see him. They did, and soon called to him. Then the French produced a white flag, indicating they wished to speak with him. He motioned for one of them to swim across the inlet, which he did. Within moments, the wet and nearly breathless French soldier stood before Menéndez.

The soldier told the governor what he already knew: The men were all survivors of a shipwreck. Then, Menéndez learned that there were more than 200 men across the bay. The French outnumbered the Spaniards four to one!

Although he already knew the answer, Menéndez asked the man whether they were Catholic or Lutheran. The man replied that they were mostly Lutheran, but insisted they were good Christians. The governor then asked what the French wanted. The man explained that his captain sent him, only "to see what people they were."[1] Menéndez said to tell his captain that "it is the Viceroy and Captain General of this country," Pedro Menéndez, appointed by the king of Spain.[2] Further, he told the man that he had found out "the day before that they were there, and the hour at which they came."[3]

The man left, but returned almost immediately. He asked if his captain and a few of his officers might come over and discuss the situation with Menéndez. The governor gave his word that the men might come talk with him in safety. Then, Menéndez sent a boat across the inlet to bring the men over.

The French captain arrived with four of his men. The governor and 10 of his soldiers greeted them. The captain told Menéndez that he and his men were unfortunate victims of a storm that had separated them from their three other ships. The storm had blown their ships onto the reef. Their ships damaged beyond repair, the men wanted to return north to their fort. The captain told Menéndez that he and his men were hungry. He also asked if he could borrow a boat to cross the inlet

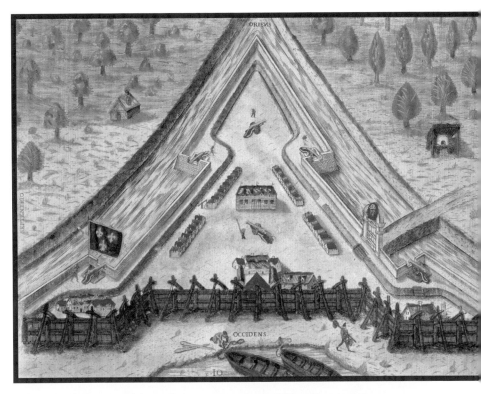

Fort Caroline, depicted in this sixteenth-century color engraving by German artist Theodore de Bry, was the first French colony in North America. Established in 1564, it was located near present-day Jacksonville, Florida, approximately 35 miles north of St. Augustine.

and then sail up the coast in order to reach his countrymen at Fort Caroline.

Menéndez listened thoughtfully to the captain as he spoke. When he finished, the governor slowly told the Frenchmen, through an interpreter, about "the capture of Fort Caroline and the slaughter of the garrison."[4] Menéndez could not see why he should help the Frenchmen go to a fort that now belonged to Spain. The captain realized it would be pointless to proceed northward. Then he reminded Menéndez that France and Spain were not at war, and that he considered the Spaniards "friends and brothers."[5] Then, he asked Menéndez for a ship in order to take his men to France.

Menéndez told the French captain that he only felt obligated to help those who were either Catholic or his friends. Because the French survivors had already admitted they belonged to the Lutheran Church, he could see no reason to help them. He then spoke very plainly to the delegation, telling them he viewed them as enemies. He shared with them an oath he had taken to "wage war upon" any Lutherans he might find on land or sea "with fire and sword."[6] He told them of his duty to bring Christianity to the Native Americans in Florida. Menéndez paused. He looked at the French captain and his advisors. They watched him intently to see what he would say next. Menéndez chose his next words carefully. He did not want to make a rash promise to his French enemies, a promise he would be forced to keep. Speaking though an interpreter, he used terms that might be understood in more than one way. Menéndez let them know that they could surrender their weapons and "yield themselves to his mercy."[7] If they did so, he pledged only that "he might do to them what should be directed him by the grace of God."[8]

The French captain and his men then returned across the inlet to confer with the other men. After a short while, the captain and his advisors returned. This time, the captain told Menéndez that his ship included wealthy men who promised to pay generously to guarantee their safety. Menéndez refused to accept money, claiming any mercy he showed should be from his heart, not out of obligation.

The French seemed to accept the negotiations were over. They could either yield to the Spanish or face starvation. Obtaining no guarantees in return for their surrender, the French captain reluctantly submitted to Menéndez. To show their good faith, all weapons were loaded into the small boat and sent across the inlet. Then, the French were brought over 10 men at a time.

Meanwhile, Menéndez kept his force just out of sight behind the sand dunes. The governor did not want the French to realize how few Spaniards were taking them prisoner. Nor could he afford to let the French realize what was about to happen. While the French returned to their side of the inlet to discuss their surrender, Menéndez went to his men, to make the necessary arrangements.

Behind the dunes and out of sight of the French force, Menéndez walked along the beach. He paused and looked around. He could not see the French from where he stood. Taking his lance, he drew a long line in the sand. His eyes met those of one of his officers. Without speaking, the officer understood the order. He, too, knew what must be done.

The first group of French soldiers arrived. Pedro Menéndez greeted them and offered them food. The half-starved men ate quickly. Then, the governor spoke to them. He admitted that there were very few Spanish soldiers there with him. Because there were more than 200 French soldiers, Pedro Menéndez proposed tying them up. Otherwise, the French might be tempted to attack and overwhelm the small group guarding them as they marched to St. Augustine.

The French soldiers quickly agreed. Soon, all 10 were standing with their arms securely tied behind their backs. Then, they waited while the second group of 10 had arrived, eaten, and agreed to have their hands tied behind their backs. The day grew hot as the boat repeatedly made its way slowly across the inlet. Each time it returned, it brought another 10 French soldiers who disembarked, ate, and were then bound. Finally, late in the day, 208 Frenchmen stood on the beach, their arms bound behind them. Menéndez asked if any among them were Catholic. Eight identified themselves as Catholic and were removed from the group. They were sent out to the small Spanish ship waiting offshore.

Then, the Spaniards began to march the Frenchmen up the beach. Within moments, they passed behind the large sand dune. As the men walked, they reached a line drawn in the sand—the line Menéndez had drawn with his lance. When the captives reached the line, the Spanish soldiers suddenly attacked the helpless Frenchmen. Without mercy, each of the men was quickly stabbed. Within moments, a mass of men lay dead, their blood soaking into the sand on the beach.

The French soldiers now lay dead on the beach. The Spanish cleaned their swords and gathered their things. As the sky darkened and stars appeared, Menéndez and his men quickly made their way back to St. Augustine. The place they left would be called *Matanzas*, which means the place of slaughter.

Only two weeks later, another group of shipwrecked French soldiers would find themselves on the south side of the inlet. This group faced the same situation. Across the bay, standing near the line in the sand, would be the same Spaniard, none other than Pedro Menéndez de Avilés, the founder of St. Augustine, Florida. The result of that meeting would determine whether France or Spain would be the dominant power over the next two centuries in St. Augustine and in Florida.

2

The Spanish Colonial Empire

EARLY EUROPEAN EXPLORATION

Many years before the massacre of French soldiers on a Florida beach, various European countries began the process of exploration that eventually led to conflicts in the New World. The history of exploration begins not with Spain, but with Portugal, Spain's small neighbor. Today, Spain and Portugal make up the Iberian Peninsula, the landmass in southwestern Europe. The peninsula's name comes "from the Ancient Greeks who called those who lived there *Iberians*. Those ancient people and the peninsula probably took their name from the peninsula's second-longest river, the Ebro [or Iberus]."[9] Early in the fifteenth century, the Portuguese began to explore Africa. Like other European nations, Portugal wanted to establish a reliable trade route with Asia. Portuguese efforts to establish this trade were focused on tapping into the overland trade routes that brought Asian products into Africa. These products included spices, silk, and tea, none of which were found in Europe.

In the early part of the fifteenth century, Portugal became the first European nation to establish an overseas trade network with Africa. The man most responsible for the creation of this empire was Prince Henry of Portugal (depicted here), who established a school for cartographers and navigators at the southwestern tip of the Iberian Peninsula, near Cape St. Vincent.

In the first half of the fifteenth century, Prince Henry the Navigator, a member of the Portuguese nobility, greatly helped his country accomplish its goals. He established a school for cartographers and navigators. A cartographer makes maps, while a navigator is a person on a ship who is responsible for planning the journey and knowing the ship's location at all times. At his school, Henry brought together the most gifted and knowledgeable men needed for overseas exploration. Now Portugal had navigators, who had firsthand experiences with sailing, working with cartographers who wanted to draw maps of ocean currents, islands, reefs, and coastlines.

Following Henry's lead, Portugal quickly increased the number of colonial settlements in Africa. With more points of access to Africa, Portugal reached the African trade routes with the Middle and Far East. Increased trade with Africa meant one thing for Portugal: wealth. The small European kingdom, located next to Spain on the Iberian Peninsula, became very prosperous.

Portuguese successes not only aided the little kingdom, but also raised the awareness of the potential benefits of colonies. Soon, other nations could not resist the allure of establishing colonies and trade with Asia. By the end of the fifteenth century, Portugal was no longer alone in its quest to create and maintain trade routes with Asia. Before long, Portugal's nearest neighbor, Spain, began to search for ways to rival Henry's homeland.

THE MOORS AND SPAIN

Spain's chance at colonial greatness came from an unlikely source: a sailor named Christopher Columbus, from the city of Genoa (in present-day Italy). Columbus had a different view of the world than other explorers at the time. He believed that one could reach the Far East by sailing west. Despite popular myths to the contrary, Columbus was not the first to reject the notion of a flat earth. Indeed, many other explorers believed the earth was round. However, Columbus did maintain that the earth was smaller than others believed.

For early explorers, the size of the earth was an essential part of planning if one intended to sail west to reach Asia. Ships at the time were much smaller than today, and an explorer could not expect to find provisions while at sea. The distance and/or length of time a ship could spend at sea depended upon how much food and water it could carry in its hold. Other navigators believed the earth was round, but they did not accept Columbus's calculations for the size of the globe.

Christopher Columbus claimed that the earth's circumference was smaller than what other navigators believed. The Genoan made a key mistake in his calculations. Because he was Italian, Columbus used the distance for miles that Italians used. But Italian miles are shorter than the miles other explorers used for their calculations. Columbus used the Italian distances in his calculations and mistakenly concluded that the world was smaller than it really is. Because he believed the earth was smaller, Columbus claimed that Asia was much closer to Europe.

Ironically, Columbus first proposed his ideas of exploration to the Portuguese. Of course, Portugal had many talented and well-trained navigators of its own. These experts realized that Columbus's proposal was flawed due to the inaccurate projections of the earth's size. Portugal thanked Columbus for his time, but turned down the proposal.

Columbus was not discouraged. Instead of giving up, he went to a growing nation that needed to do something bold to enhance its power. That nation was Spain. At the end of the fifteenth century, Spain was perfectly poised to take advantage of Columbus's offer to find a new trade route to Asia. Ferdinand of Aragon and Isabella of Castile married in 1469 and united the two largest Spanish kingdoms within 10 years. However, not all was well within Spain. The nation had been ravaged by war for many years.

Starting in the early 700s A.D., the Iberian Peninsula was invaded by people from North Africa. These intruders were Arab Muslims, or Moors. The Moors extended their territory into Europe. Crossing the Mediterranean Sea near Gibraltar, they successfully captured most of the Iberian Peninsula by A.D. 718 However, the Moors never completely conquered all of the Christian kingdoms on the Iberian Peninsula. Thus, for nearly 400 years, the mountainous region of the north was the only part of Spain that remained free of Moorish control.

The Moors ruled most of Spain and established their capital city in Córdoba. Situated in southern Spain, Córdoba was a vital city positioned on the Guadalquivir River, an important waterway. Under Moorish rule, architecture, arts, and literature flourished. The Moors undertook massive construction projects, building mosques (Muslim places of worship) and castles (called alcazars). The Moors also kept and cared for ancient Greek, Latin, and Middle Eastern writings. Before the Spanish again controlled the peninsula, the richness of Moorish scholarship attracted intellectuals from across Europe. Amazingly, the Moors tolerated individuals from a variety of faiths. Jews and Christians were allowed to live and work in Moorish society. In fact, some of these non-Muslims contributed to the thriving culture of the Moors.

As their culture flourished, the Moors' military strength declined. Their central power grew ineffective, unable to compel obedience from the smaller, independent Moorish cities and states. Then, one of the strengths of the Moorish system of government came unraveled: the structure of local government. Since arriving in Spain, the Moors allowed local matters to be decided by the local authorities—even if those

In A.D. 707, Muslim Moors from North Africa began their conquest
of Spain when they invaded the island of Mallorca, which is depicted
in this fresco by an unknown Arab artist from the thirteenth century.
Four years later, the Moors invaded the mainland and within less than
a decade, they controlled most of the Iberian Peninsula.

authorities happened to be citizens of a Christian kingdom. As the power of the centralized Moorish government lessened, these Christian kingdoms grew increasingly intolerant of Moorish rule.

Eventually, the Christian kingdoms under Moorish control gained strength. They started challenging the Moors and recovering parts of Spain. Leading the fight against the Moors was the Christian kingdom of Castile, located in north-central Spain. Castile desired to force the Moors off the Iberian Peninsula. Initially, the Christian kingdoms were limited to northern Spain. Slowly, the Christian kingdoms enlarged their control until they held most of the land in northern Spain from the Mediterranean Sea in the east to the Atlantic Ocean in the west. In time, the Moors were driven southward, toward the Strait of Gibraltar.

Military triumphs helped Castile grow more powerful among the Christian kingdoms. Other kingdoms, however, resented Castilian leadership. One of these other kingdoms successfully broke away from Castile, winning its independence during the twelfth century. This kingdom became known as Portugal. The Portuguese controlled all of their modern territory by the middle of the thirteenth century.

In order to enlist more support and coordinate their war efforts, the various Christian kingdoms started meeting together. These gatherings were essentially a parliament, which they called a *Cortes*. The Cortes included delegates from the nobility and the Catholic Church. The body also included representatives from the Spanish middle class. Although kings held most of the power within each kingdom, the Cortes helped expand support against the Moors.

Throughout the twelfth and thirteenth centuries, the Christian kingdoms steadily pushed the Moors farther and farther southward on the Iberian Peninsula. By the late 1200s, the Christian kingdoms ruled all but the small kingdom of

By the early thirteenth century, Muslim control of Spain had been reduced to the Kingdom of Granada, in the southern part of the country. The Moors were not forced to surrender Granada until Spain was united under Queen Isabella I of Castile and King Ferdinand II of Aragon in 1492. The last Moorish king, Boadbil, is depicted here surrendering to Isabella and Ferdinand.

Granada on the southern tip of Spain. The Moors' task became increasingly more difficult as the Spanish kingdoms continued to unite. This process of unification meant there were fewer kingdoms, but those few kingdoms had more control over the resources needed for war. The consolidations continued until, by 1300, there were only the three Spanish kingdoms of Aragon, Castile, and Navarre.

Of the three, Castile was the largest and the most powerful. Castile controlled most of Christian Spain. The smallest of the three, Navarre, was situated in northern Spain near the mountains. The last Christian kingdom, Aragon, held the Balearic Islands, located in the Mediterranean Sea, and most of eastern Spain. Then, the marriage of King Ferdinand of Aragon to Queen Isabella of Castile united the two largest Christian kingdoms in Spain. Within 10 years, the two ruled their combined territories as one nation. Ferdinand wanted to unify all of Spain under one flag. As for Navarre, the tiny kingdom retained its independence until Castile conquered it in 1512. In that year, all of Spain was subject to one king.

The united provinces of Castile and Aragon battled with the Spanish Muslims, or Moors, for control of Spain. The Catholic Spaniards eventually gained the upper hand, driving the Moors from the Iberian Peninsula in January 1492. Because religious differences between the Spaniards and Moors were so strong, it is of little surprise that Ferdinand and Isabella also expelled any Jews from Spain who would not convert to Christianity. Having expelled the threat from within his borders, Ferdinand wanted to expand his country beyond Europe. For his inspiration, the Spanish king needed to look no further than next door to Portugal. The tiny European nation had already enriched itself with ivory, gold, and even slaves through trading with Africa.

SPANISH EXPLORATION

Ferdinand was well aware of the prevailing opinion: Columbus was wrong—the earth simply had to be larger than he claimed. But the Spanish king also believed that the chance of finding a new sea route to Asia was worth the risk of sending Columbus on his journey. Although Columbus and Ferdinand did not know it, two continents, North and South America, lay between Spain and Asia. Fortunately for Columbus and Ferdinand, North and South America were situated approximately where Columbus believed Asia to be. Thus, while Columbus believed he had found a new route to the Far East, he actually discovered a new continent.

The Spanish monarchs did not seem to care that Columbus had found something other than a route to Asia. This indifference is easy to understand, because Christopher Columbus's voyage to the West Indies opened the door for Spain to become a major power. For Spain, the opportunity now existed to develop a profitable trade empire with the Americas. Columbus died in

PORTUGUESE OR SPANISH?

At the conclusion of his voyage, Christopher Columbus made a report to Ferdinand and Isabella. The monarchs received him by holding a large celebration. Many were eager to hear the details of his trip. Although Columbus did not have much, he did show what he could: a number of gold trinkets and a few Indians he had brought back with him.

Despite the scantiness of true wealth and power, Spain's king and queen were convinced that the opportunities to gain both were at hand. Then, they went about protecting Columbus's discovery. Ferdinand and Isabella petitioned Pope Alexander VI, asking him to grant them control over the lands Christopher Columbus had found. In addition, Spain stated its intention to teach Christianity to the native peoples of this new land. Portugal was unhappy both with Columbus's discovery and attempts to expand Spanish trade. The Portuguese argued that because they already had established trade routes, they, and not the Spanish, should control this new path for trade. The pope did not want to see the countries go to war, so he agreed to meet with Portuguese and Spanish representatives. The meetings took place in Tordesillas, Spain. There, Alexander VI negotiated a compromise between the two Catholic kingdoms. The pact, signed in 1494, was known as the Treaty of Tordesillas.

Essentially, Portugal and Spain agreed to divide the world between the two nations. The Portuguese felt their existing claims in Africa were threatened by Spain's discovery. The Spanish believed they had discovered either a

1506 still believing his journey had opened the way for trade with Asia. His sponsors, however, quickly developed an effective empire based in the West Indies, or the Caribbean islands. Over the next several decades, this trade transferred large amounts of gold and silver from Mexico and Peru to Spain. With this newfound wealth, Spain eclipsed Portugal as the preeminent European colonial power. This dominance lasted until the end of the sixteenth century.

new route to Asia or possibly some previously undiscovered islands, or both. The treaty attempted to reconcile the two sides by drawing precise lines to distinguish Spanish claims from Portuguese claims. Portugal held the Cape Verde Islands off the western coast of Africa, and these islands became the baseline for the agreement. The treaty specified that Portugal controlled all land up to 370 leagues (1,110 nautical miles or 2,056 kilometers) west of the Cape Verde Islands. Prior to this, the Portuguese claimed territory only about 100 leagues (300 nautical miles or 556 kilometers) west of the Cape Verde Islands. Thus, the settlement significantly expanded Portuguese claims.

The Treaty of Tordesillas resulted in at least two significant outcomes. First, Pope Alexander VI succeeded in averting war between the countries. Without the threat of war, Spain successfully explored and claimed large parts of Central and South America over the next 50 years. Second, the treaty dictated which countries influenced which parts of the New World, especially South America. Under the agreement, the eastern portion of South America fell under the control of Portugal. Thus, it was the Portuguese, not the Spanish, who established the colony of Brazil. Also, due to the treaty, Spain was recognized as the power in South and Central America. The effect of the Treaty of Tordesillas may today be seen in the predominant languages: In Brazil, Portuguese is the main language, whereas Spanish is the primary language in the rest of South and Central America.

3

Discovering Florida

Following Columbus's 1492 voyage, Spain initiated a series of expeditions to the Caribbean over the next several years. These early voyages of exploration led the Spanish south and westward. Thus, Florida was discovered at a much later date than Mexico and other lands claimed by Spain. As one historian stated, "Even the shores of the vast Pacific had been reached by Balboa before the southeastern portion of the United States had been discovered."[10] In short, Spanish America grew, but failed to include any of the present-day United States for decades. Hernando Cortez conquered the Aztecs of Mexico in 1521. In 1531, Francisco Pizarro triumphed over the Inca Empire in Peru. Spain controlled virtually all of Central and much of South America, as well as the islands of the Caribbean before a single Spaniard set foot on Florida's soil. But all of that changed with Juan Ponce de León, a young Spanish adventurer who wanted to discover new lands for his king and church.

Ponce de Leon.

Kapitel VIII.

Spanish conquistador Juan Ponce de León was named governor of Puerto Rico by King Ferdinand II in 1506 but was replaced by Christopher Columbus's son Diego in 1512. After he was removed from office, Ponce de León was given permission by Ferdinand to explore the lands north of Cuba, and in 1513, he became the first European to set foot in what is today Florida.

PONCE DE LEÓN

Juan Ponce de León first left Spain for the New World in 1493, when historians believe he accompanied Christopher Columbus on his second journey to the West Indies. After arriving, "Juan Ponce de León vanished from the records of the New World for nearly a decade."[11] Not much is known about the explorer after his first trip to the Caribbean. Some historians question whether he really went to the island of Hispaniola—today, Haiti and the Dominican Republic comprise the island—Spain's first colony in the New World. Others believe he went with Columbus, but then immediately returned to Spain. What historians do agree on is that, in 1502, Ponce de León resurfaced in records and soon made a name for himself.

In 1502, the island of Hispaniola was in the midst of an Indian revolt. Ponce de León became prominent through his ability to lead and fight. As compensation for his efforts, King Ferdinand II named Ponce de León governor of the eastern part of the island of Puerto Rico (called San Juan at the time). There, he managed to become quite wealthy through farming. He might have settled down and enjoyed a comfortable life; instead, Ponce de León faced a lengthy legal battle. The title of governor legally belonged to Diego Columbus, a son of the famed explorer. Diego did not intend to lose such a valuable prize and took his claim to the highest court in Spain's capital of Madrid. In 1511, the courts agreed with Columbus. As a result, Ponce de León was removed as governor, but he retained his post as the military commander of the island. The explorer might have once again faded from memory, but rumors of a rich and mysterious island to the north proved enticing. It was then that Ponce de León decided to investigate the rumors for himself. The deposed governor seemed to brighten at the prospect of new discoveries. It only made sense that Ponce de León would end up leaving San Juan. He could not rule there, and it seemed unlikely he would ever get a chance to hold any important office there. According to one historian, the prospect of "seeking and conquering a new island" was simply irresistible to Ponce de León.[12]

La Florida

In early 1512, King Ferdinand signed a contract with Juan Ponce de León. The agreement gave the adventurer permission "to explore, settle, and govern" whatever lands north of Cuba that were unoccupied by Spain.[13] Many believed that the mystical island of Bimini lay in the region northwest of Hispaniola. The commission was an open invitation to discover and conquer new lands. Ponce de León immediately made plans to leave. In March 1513, Ponce de León commanded three ships and about 65 men to search for the island of Bimini.

The purpose of his mission was to discover new lands in order to establish colonies there. The legend that has often been recorded is that Ponce de León went in search of a so-called fountain of youth. The tale of a fountain with its age-defying qualities was indeed told, but it "was no more than a secondary motivation for the voyage."[14] Perhaps the myth began, as historian George R. Fairbanks believes, as "a poetic and exaggerated description of the country."[15]

Ponce de León first saw the coast of what he believed was a large island on Palm Sunday, called *Pascua Florida*, Spanish for Easter of the Flowers. Observing the date and the colorful vegetation on the mainland, the explorer appropriately named the new land *La Florida*—the Flowered One. Landing ashore, Ponce de León carried out the "usual ceremony of planting a cross and taking possession of the country in the name of the Spanish monarch."[16]

For two months, Ponce de León and his party investigated the land. They also sailed along the coast, occasionally

Although Juan Ponce de León is often depicted in his search for the fabled fountain of youth, in reality, he ventured to Florida to claim lands for Spain and look for gold. The story of Ponce de León's search for the fountain of youth most likely surfaced in the *Memoir of Hernando de Escalante Fontaneda* in the 1560s.

weighing anchor and exploring parts of this unknown land. All the while, Ponce de León was still convinced that Florida was an island. During those two months, interaction with the natives was less than desirable. In the eyes of the Spaniards, the Native Americans were aggressive and ruthless. After spending weeks in a fruitless search for gold and perhaps a magical fountain, the expedition returned to Puerto Rico.

Upon his return, Ponce de León told of his discovery, and boasted that the land was full of riches. His account became widely known, gaining him a great deal of fame. In 1514, the king authorized Ponce de León to colonize "the island of Florida."[17] The Crown also allowed the explorer to govern whatever land he conquered. Ponce de León also was told by the king to take priests with him in order "to convert them to our Holy Catholic Faith."[18] Although Ponce de León could now return to Florida, it took seven years for him to mount another expedition.

THE END OF PONCE DE LEÓN

Ponce de León again made plans to leave for Florida in 1521. Since the time he had discovered it, another Spanish explorer, Alonzo Álvarez de Pineda, learned in 1519 that Florida was not an island, but a peninsula. Cruising near the coast at what is now the Mobile River and Bay, Pineda determined that land that was thought to be an island was connected to the mainland. He named the river Río de Espíritu Santo, in honor of the Holy Spirit.

Finally, Ponce de León left Puerto Rico in 1521 with two ships bearing "two hundred men and fifty horses, together with a variety of domestic animals" and tools needed for farming.[19] This time, the expedition also included several priests. When they landed in Florida with the expedition, it is believed that they were the first Catholic priests to set foot in what is now the United States.

Historians do not know exactly where the party landed in July 1521, perhaps near Charlotte Harbor (on the Gulf Coast). What is known is the party received a rather rude and harsh welcome. Local Native Americans met the group almost immediately, and they were heavily armed. The Indians attacked, killing many in the landing party. An arrow struck Ponce de León, badly wounding him. The Spaniards rallied around their leader, taking him to the safety of a ship. Realizing the wound was serious, Ponce de León insisted the ships return him to

THE GULF STREAM

Perhaps the most important discovery Juan Ponce de León made on his voyage to Florida was the Gulf Stream. The Gulf Stream is essentially a "vast river within the ocean" that flows north through the Gulf of Mexico.* Spanish historian Antonio de Herrera y Tordesillas wrote about this discovery about 90 years after the voyage. The ships, Herrera wrote, "encountered a current that they were unable to sail against even though they had a strong wind."** After passing through the Straits of Florida, the current travels up the coast all the way to Nantucket Island off the coast of Massachusetts before flowing east to Europe. The Gulf Stream "moves as much as four billion tons of water a minute at speeds up to five miles per hour near Palm Beach, Florida."*** At this point, the volume of its flow is "a thousand times greater than that of the Mississippi River."[†] Ponce de León reported his discovery of the great *corriente*, or current, when he returned to Puerto Rico (San Juan) in 1513. Almost as soon as the Spanish learned of it, they recognized its importance. Whereas Columbus had found the trade winds to sail west, Ponce de León had found the means to return quickly to Europe. Some historians believe that finding the Gulf Stream was the most important European discovery following that of Columbus's voyage when he used the prevailing northeast trade winds to sail west to the New World. Together, these two discoveries influenced North Atlantic sea traffic for the next three centuries. Only the introduction of the steam-powered ship altered these established routes of sea travel, because such ships could travel against the current. Indeed, even modern ships take advantage of the winds and currents when possible.

Ironically, the location of the Gulf Stream near the Florida coast later influenced Pedro Menéndez de Avilés as he searched for a suitable site for his colony. A natural harbor on the coast was necessary for a successful colony, but finding a place near the Gulf Stream was even more important. With such a location, large ships could easily supply the fort and provide protection for the Spanish galleons filled with shipments of gold and silver from Mexico and Peru.

---

  * Robert Fuson, *Juan Ponce de Leon and the Spanish Discovery of Puerto Rico and Florida* (Blacksburg, Va.: The MacDonald and Woodward Publishing Company, 2000), 120.

 ** Louise Chipley Slavicek, *Juan Ponce de Leon* (Philadelphia: Chelsea House Publishers, 2003), 74–75.

*** Fuson, 120.

  † Ibid.

Cuba, where he might receive better medical treatment. Unfortunately, his wounds were too severe and Ponce de León died from the injuries a few days later in Havana.

Thus, the Ponce de León era in Florida came to an end before it really began. The task of establishing a colony on the unforgiving peninsula now belonged to others. These later explorers faced many of the same difficulties that dashed the dreams of Juan Ponce de León, the Spanish discoverer of Florida.

4

Spanish Failures in Florida

After the death of Juan Ponce de León, several Spanish explor-ers attempted to establish colonies in Florida. Each time, the expeditions either met hostile Native Americans or faced insurmountable weather conditions. Regardless of the cause for failure, these expeditions fell short of the Spanish dream to colonize Florida.

THE AYLLÓN EXPEDITION

In 1526, Lucas Vásquez de Ayllón tried to do what Ponce de León could not. Ayllón was a Crown-appointed judge serving in Santo Domingo on the island of Hispaniola in the Caribbean. The judge decided to mount an expedition to Florida. When he set sail, he had a massive group accompanying him: "600 men and women, including two priests."[20] They sailed north along the eastern coast of Florida, finally choosing to land in the vicinity of Winyah Bay in present-day South Carolina, on September 29, 1526. At that time, the entire North American eastern seaboard was considered part of Florida.

The group landed their provisions and began building homes and a church. Before long, the settlers began running out of food. The shortage of food was complicated by the onset of winter. Disease and sickness accompanied the cooler weather. Ayllón himself fell ill and succumbed. The expedition leader "died in the arms" of one of the priests.[21] Upon his death just three months after landing, only about 150 discouraged colonists remained, and they were tired of the cold and hunger. The disheartened group chose to leave, returning to Santo Domingo during that first winter. The Ayllón expedition, which had held so much promise when it began, ended in failure.

THE NARVÁEZ EXPEDITION

In 1527, Pánfilo de Narváez, a Spaniard, led an expedition to Florida, where he planned to establish a colony. Narváez landed on Florida's west coast probably near present-day Tampa Bay. He had with him at least 300 men. Shortly after landing, Narváez sent his ships back to Mexico. Left alone on the mainland without the means to leave, the group explored along the coast and inland. The expedition searched for gold, but did not find any. Narváez's men often treated the local natives cruelly, which led to warfare. Indians killed some of the men. Disease claimed the lives of others. Narváez and his men lacked the necessary supplies to support themselves, especially food. Facing starvation, "the men killed their horses in order to eat."[22] Narváez finally admitted failure and decided to abandon the venture.

But, the expedition did not have any ships and had no way to leave Florida. In order to escape their fate, the men built crude boats. They set sail into the Gulf of Mexico. Once they left the shore, severe storms struck the small boats. The boats became

After sailing from Spain in June 1527, Pánfilo de Narváez finally reached Florida the following February and explored the region around present-day Tampa Bay, before heading inland in search of gold. Unfortunately for Narváez and his crew, they were stranded after their ships failed to return to pick them up.

separated. Some sank, and the men on board drowned. Other boats were carried out to sea and were never seen again. A single boat survived. In it was Alvar Núñez Cabeza de Vaca. He and the others in his boat eventually "landed on a small island off the coast of Texas, near present-day Galveston" late in the fall.[23]

The few remaining members of the Narváez expedition would have died, but local Native Americans took them in and cared for them. Both the Native Americans and the Spaniards faced starvation that winter. Lack of food and disease thinned the ranks of the Indians and Spaniards alike. When spring arrived, only 15 remained from the Narváez expedition. Unfortunately for these few survivors, their troubles were not over.

Some of the Native Americans blamed the Spaniards for the starvation and disease that had inflicted losses on their own people. This led some of the natives to distrust the strangers. Some members of the tribe did not think it was wise to continue helping the Spaniards. The expedition survivors recognized their fragile situation. They "needed to make themselves useful" to the Native Americans.[24] Cabeza de Vaca, at the opportune time, acted as if he was a medicine man. He imitated the Indian medicine man by waving his hands over the sick and reciting chants. Although Cabeza de Vaca doubted his own abilities to heal, the Native Americans were convinced. His impersonation saved his life.

For several years, the few remaining Spaniards fought to remain alive. They did whatever it took to survive. "They pretended to be medicine men. They helped the Native Americans trade. They worked as slaves. All the while, they thought about getting back to New Spain."[25]

Finally, after years of suffering, only five from the Narváez expedition survived. The men discussed traveling south and west to reach New Spain. Four decided to try, while the fifth rejected the idea. The other four left him with the Native Americans. The four men began walking southwest, making contact with Spanish slave hunters a year later. The four survivors were Alvar Núñez Cabeza de Vaca, Andres de Caranca, Alonzo Castillo Maldonado, and a slave named Estevanico (usually called by his Spanish name of Esteban). When they appeared in Mexico City, they were quite a sight. The four men were hungry and dirty. Each wore a long beard. They were thin and obviously half-starved. Their clothes were worn and filthy, made of animal "skins and tattered cloth."[26] But they were alive. And their arrival in Mexico City in the summer of 1536 led to yet another Spanish expedition in search of fabled gold. This time, Francisco Coronado led an expedition to the American Southwest in 1540.

As for the other members of the Narváez expedition, no one knows for sure what happened to them. In Florida history, Narváez is simply one in a list of distinguished Spaniards who failed to establish a colony there.

THE SATURIBA INDIANS

When early explorers reached Florida, the Native Americans they encountered were often quick to attack the European strangers. The Native Americans near the future St. Augustine were the Saturibas. These Native Americans spoke a dialect of Timucuan, an Indian language spoken by as many as a dozen tribes from southeastern Georgia to northeastern Florida.

Ruling the Saturibas was a great chief. Governing each village was a lesser chief who owed his allegiance to the tribal chief. All chiefs were viewed as nobility and related to one another. Other members of clans in high standing made up the chief's advisors.

Members of the upper class also decorated their bodies with elaborate tattoos, colored red, blue, and black. The tribe used dyes that were pricked into the skin. Nobility and commoners wore hardly any coverings, but did paint their bodies for special ceremonies and warfare. Other forms of decoration included feathers, shell jewelry, and occasionally jewelry made of copper, gold, or silver.

The Saturibas raised crops of corn, beans, pumpkin, and squash in addition to gathering wild fruits and vegetables. They also relied on fish and game to supplement their diet. Sixteenth-century French artist Jacques LeMoyne observed the Saturibas while serving at Fort Caroline, the French fort located several miles north of St. Augustine. LeMoyne sketched drawings of the local natives while in Florida. He also described their unique hunting techniques in this way:

> The Indians hunt deer in a way we have never seen before. They hide themselves in the skin of a very large deer which they have killed some time before. They place the animal's head upon their own head, looking through the eye holes as through a mask. In this disguise they approach the deer without frightening them.*

THE DE SOTO EXPEDITION

The next to try his luck in Florida was 38-year-old Hernando de Soto, a knight in the Order of Santiago. De Soto had served under the command of Francisco Pizarro in 1531, when Pizarro

The Saturibas relied more heavily on hunted game during the lean winter months. These hunter-gatherers were the natives that greeted Pedro Menéndez de Avilés when he founded St. Augustine.

* John W. Griffin, *The Men Who Met Menendez: 8000 B.C.—1562 A.D.*, as found in Jean Parker Waterbury, ed., *The Oldest City: St. Augustine, Saga of Survival* (St. Augustine, Fla.: The St. Augustine Historical Society, 1983), 16.

German artist Theodore de Bry modeled this engraving after a drawing by French artist Jacques LeMoyne, who made sketches of local Indian tribes while he was at Fort Caroline with Jean Ribault's expedition. Here, hunters are depicted in deerskins in pursuit of their quarry.

conquered the Inca Empire in Peru. Under Pizarro, the young officer proved himself a capable and daring leader. De Soto resolved to "conquer, pacify, and populate" Florida and the region lying to the west, all the way to the Rio Grande in 1538.[27] The task before him seemed overwhelming, especially considering the outcome of expeditions under de León, de Ayllón, and Narváez. But de Soto was determined to succeed where others had failed.

The young adventurer left Spain on April 6, 1538. His 620 men and supplies were in 10 ships. His party included 12 priests "for the instruction of the natives."[28] De Soto tarried in Cuba for nearly a year, gathering additional supplies for his undertaking. Finally, on May 25, 1539, he reached the west coast of Florida, at the same place Narváez had disembarked on his ill-fated trip. On June 3, de Soto landed, following all the formalities in taking possession of the land.

Shortly after landing, the party found a fellow Spaniard, a survivor of a group that had searched for the Narváez expedition and been captured by Native Americans. The man had lived as a captive for 11 years. His name was Juan Ortíz, and he served as de Soto's interpreter in Florida. Through Ortíz and natives who spoke more than one language, de Soto was able to communicate with other tribes as he journeyed north and west. Whenever the Spaniards encountered a new language, they simply found a native who knew the language they were leaving as well as the one they were encountering. By the time he reached the Mississippi River in 1542, de Soto's "words would have to pass through more than a dozen people before they reached the intended recipient."[29]

De Soto sent most of the ships back to Cuba to avoid a mutiny or desertions. After having already faced some dangers, some members of the party volunteered to return with the ships. This group even included Vasco Porcallo de Figueroa, de Soto's

Following the failed mission of Pánfilo de Narváez, Hernando de Soto set out to establish a colony in western Florida in 1539. However, de Soto was more interested in exploring the vast new land, and over the following few years, he and his party traveled extensively throughout what is today the southeastern part of the United States.

lieutenant general. A Native American shot Figueroa's horse with an arrow while he rode it. Instead of pursuing the life of an adventurer, Figueroa returned to his Cuban estate.

The expedition did not linger long in Florida. Soon, the party made its way north and west, exploring parts of the future American states of Florida, Georgia, South and North Carolina, Tennessee, Alabama, Mississippi, Arkansas, Louisiana, and Texas. De Soto died from a fever in May 1542, but not before he discovered for Europe the greatest river in North America: the Mississippi. After he died, his men buried him in the mighty river.

Once again, despite all the planning and preparation, an attempt to colonize Florida had failed. This time, the failure probably had more to do with the ambitiousness of the leader. The expedition was more intent on exploration and possibly discovering gold than on setting up a settlement. Even so, the abilities and resources of Don Hernando de Soto meant his expedition included many of the elements needed for success. The de Soto expedition was another wasted opportunity for Spain to establish itself in Florida.

OTHER ATTEMPTS TO COLONIZE FLORIDA

In 1549, the Spanish tried again to establish a colony in Florida. This time, they took a nonviolent approach. The Spanish sent Catholic missionaries to the west coast. The team consisted of five Dominican friars. The undertaking failed when Native Americans murdered one of the missionaries, Fray Luis Cancer de Barbastro.

A decade later, the Spanish launched a bold effort at establishing a colony. Tristán de Luna y Arellano led a group from Mexico to Pensacola Bay. The expedition was composed of 13 ships. On the ships were more than 1,000 colonists and 500 soldiers. The ships also carried all the necessary equipment, food, and supplies for the massive undertaking. The ships arrived at Pensacola Bay in August 1559. The colonists landed, but then disaster struck when a hurricane hit. The ships still held the essential supplies. After the storm ended, the damage was found to be disastrous for the colony. The well-planned and almost perfectly executed expedition ended as had all the other attempts to establish a Florida colony—in failure.

The Spanish monarch, Philip II, decided enough was enough. In 1561, the Crown mandated that no more attempts be made to colonize Florida. The natives were unfriendly, the climate too harsh, the risks too great. Florida simply was not meant to be colonized. It was not long, however, before the Spanish king had a change of heart. An ambitious and talented Spanish seaman and the threat of another country establishing a colony in Florida led to a reversal in Spanish policy. Soon, the Spanish were going to try again to settle *La Florida*.

5

Pedro Menéndez de Avilés

The story of St. Augustine cannot be told without including the story of its founder, Pedro Menéndez de Avilés. Menéndez was born on February 15, 1519. He was one of 20 children and was one of the youngest in his large family. Pedro was born in the town of Avilés, Spain. Avilés is located in Asturias, a region on the coast of northern Spain. Asturias is made up of mountainous terrain and this region never submitted to the Moors.

The future founder of St. Augustine came from an important Spanish family. Pedro's father was Juan Alphonso Sánchez de Avilés. As a young man, Juan Alphonso fought under King Ferdinand and Queen Isabella against the Moors. In early 1492, Spanish forces defeated the last of the Moors. Spain was free to pursue other ventures, including establishing an empire in the Americas. Juan Alphonso's son later became an important figure in extending that empire to include Florida.

Pedro Menéndez de Avilés, who later founded St. Augustine, was born in Avilés, Spain, in 1519, and was the son of Juan Alphonso Sánchez de Avilés. At the age of 14, Pedro left his home and began a life on the high seas, and by the time he was 35, he had achieved the rank of captain general of the Fleet of the Indies.

THE EARLY LIFE OF
ST. AUGUSTINE'S FOUNDER

Pedro was only a boy when his father died. Although the family name was indeed a noble one, the family lacked adequate income. Pedro's mother, Maria Alonso de Arango, remarried. Because she still did not have enough money to feed the family, Pedro was sent to live with a relative. Just eight years old, Pedro refused to give in to the chaotic changes being forced upon him. Wanting to resist the unwelcome changes, he ran away from home. For six months he wandered, begged, and scraped out an existence without his family to help him. Finally, his family found him and brought him back home.

But the youth simply refused to submit to his circumstances. Headstrong, independent, and persistent, Pedro was determined to make something of his life. His family, sensing the boy's determination, signed a marriage contract for him, pledging the youth to wed the then 10-year-old Ana María, whom he later married.

A LIFE AT SEA

Despite his family's attempt to control Pedro's life, independence drove the young boy. At 14, Pedro ran away again, this time to the sea. He signed on to a Spanish ship setting sail to fight French pirates. It was on a ship and at sea where Pedro the boy became a man. When he turned 16, Pedro returned home to claim his inheritance. Ignoring the advice of family members and his fiancée, he sold part of his inheritance, and then invested the money in a new ship. Menéndez intended to make a living by fighting French pirates. Years later, he would make a name for himself through his dealings with French pirates in the New World.

On the sea, Menéndez was fearless, relentless, and quickly made a reputation for himself. He bravely fought corsairs

(French pirates) even when outnumbered and outgunned. He gained many victories over the marauding pirates of the high seas. He once drove off four French ships attacking a wedding celebration aboard a ship. Menéndez had only one ship, but captured two ships before the other two fled.

In 1554, King Charles V appointed the 35-year-old Menéndez to escort the crown prince, Philip (later Philip II), to England to marry Queen Mary I. The same year, the Spanish Crown bestowed another honor upon the young sea captain: captain general of the Fleet of the Indies. Menéndez was responsible for protecting Spanish treasure ships as they returned to Spain from the New World. King Philip II ascended to the throne of Spain in 1556 and continued to rely on the talents of the gifted captain from Avilés.

In 1559, Menéndez was stricken with a fever that nearly killed him. He struggled with the lingering effects of the mysterious illness for several months. In 1560, Philip once again appointed him captain general of the Fleet of the Indies. Menéndez accepted the post that year and again the following year. While he held this position, Menéndez successfully won many battles over pirates, and he grew very wealthy.

Despite his successes, not everyone in Spain was pleased with the exploits of Captain Menéndez. Some criticized the captain, claiming he was nothing more than a pirate himself. Some were jealous of his achievements. Unfortunately for Menéndez, some of these critics were influential members of the king's court. They accused Menéndez of misusing his position to smuggle and make extra money aside from his royal salary. These rivals had enough power to throw Menéndez and his brother Bartolomé into prison in August 1563. They languished there for 18 months, waiting for a trial that never came.

Historians disagree over the merit of the charges. Some say Menéndez did in fact take unfair advantage of his position.

Others argue that the charges were simply the result of Menéndez becoming too powerful and popular, thereby threatening the power of his enemies. Whatever the case, the charges against Pedro Menéndez remained unproven and he was released in February 1565. However, the court did fine him. As if to demonstrate his belief in the innocence of Menéndez, King Philip II met with his former captain general of the Indies shortly after his release from prison. The king was looking for a man to lead an extraordinary mission, a mission to a place where so many others had failed. In Menéndez, it appeared that Spain finally had the kind of man needed to establish a successful colony in Florida. Philip believed Menéndez was just the man he needed. And in 1562, the seaman from Avilés embarked on yet another incredible journey, this time to the untamed lands of Florida.

COMPETITION FOR FLORIDA

Spanish explorer Juan Ponce de León first set foot on Florida soil in 1513. He claimed Florida for his country, and Spain regarded the territory as part of its overseas empire. After Ponce de León discovered Florida, Spain sent expedition after expedition to settle the region. Each expedition failed to establish a colony there. Although weather, climate, and maintaining supplies were problems, the biggest obstacle was the native population. Apparently, the local Native Americans did not want the Spanish to start a settlement there. The Spanish became worn out from their efforts. Finally, King Philip II proclaimed in September 1561 that Spain no longer intended to set up a colony in Florida. Events outside Philip's control, however, soon resulted in Spain's return to Florida.

France, one of Spain's rivals, decided to challenge the Spanish in the New World. Because Spain seemed uninterested in Florida, France became resolved to establish itself as the power

French explorer Jean Ribault's expedition to what would later become the southeastern U.S. coast is depicted in this 1590 line engraving by Theodore de Bry. Among Ribault's many accomplishments was the "discovery" of the River Mai, known today as the St. Johns River.

in the region. In 1562, Jean Ribault led a French expedition along the Florida coastline. Ribault discovered the mouth of a river the French called the River Mai (now called the St. Johns River). Ribault and his men set up a stone column made of marble, which claimed the land for France. In 1564, René de Laudonnière led another French expedition that sailed up the same river and established a colony near present-day Jacksonville. They called this colony Fort Caroline. The French military presence at this fort would later become the focus of conflict between the French and Spanish in Florida.

There was yet another underlying reason for the tensions between the French and Spanish expeditions—religion. The French expeditions were made up primarily of Lutherans. That is, the French soldiers were Protestants, called Huguenots in France. Pedro Menéndez and his men, however, were devout Catholics. The story of Spanish conquests in the New World is closely linked to the spread of Catholicism to the native

EVANGELIZING THE NATIVE AMERICANS OF FLORIDA

Throughout the sixteenth and seventeenth centuries, Spanish expeditions usually included at least one Catholic priest. These priests offered spiritual guidance and performed religious functions for the expedition members. More importantly, these men of the cloth also served as missionaries for the native peoples they encountered.

The inclusion of priests in the expeditions was important to Spanish kings. As a rule, the contracts awarding an adventurer the right to explore, settle, and/or conquer a territory also required the explorer to take priests on the journey. The expressed purpose of these additional party members was to convert the Native Americans.

But converting Native Americans in Florida proved to be a difficult task. The Native Americans there treated the priests the same way they treated the Spanish explorers: with open hostility. A well-known mission effort led by the Spanish priest Luis Cancer ended in the violent death of the peaceful cleric. Cancer died on the beach, praying for the souls of the Native Americans even as they struck him down.

Amazingly, it was a man accustomed to warfare who enjoyed the most success in peacefully converting Florida's tribes. Pedro Menéndez de Avilés stands almost alone in his success in establishing friendly relations with the natives. When he first entered a village, the governor offered the hand of friendship, shared food, and gave gifts to the natives. Then, he asked for, and always received, permission to erect a cross in a prominent place within the village. This method proved to be very effective. As Catholic priests later followed in the footsteps of Menéndez, a cross marked the spot for many future churches.

populations. Thus, the conflict between Menéndez and Ribault is not surprising.

The establishment of a French fort also drove the Spanish to alter their policy. Once he realized the extent of French presence in Florida, Philip II changed his mind and made plans to establish a Spanish colony there. Motivated in part by hatred for French defections from the Catholic Church, Philip appointed "Pedro Menéndez de Avilés, a brave bigoted, and remorseless soldier, to drive out the French colony and take possession of the country for himself."[30] Officially, Spain's monarch appointed Pedro Menéndez the governor of Florida—even though the Spanish did not yet have a single established colony there. Philip also told Governor Menéndez, "If there be settlers or corsairs of other nations . . . drive them out."[31]

As was customary, the appointment was ratified in the form of a contract between Philip and Menéndez. The agreement required Menéndez to "furnish one galleon completely equipped, and provisions for a force of six hundred men."[32] He was commissioned to "conquer and settle the country" in the name of Philip II.[33]

In keeping with Spanish tradition, Menéndez also took priests with him. Philip expected the priests of the colony to teach and convert the local population to the Roman Catholic faith. Most importantly, Philip gave Menéndez permission to fight and kill any Lutherans he might encounter in Florida. Because the only Lutherans who might be in Florida were French, Menéndez was destined to clash with the French colonists already there. Thus, the animosity Menéndez later showed to the French was simply a carryover of Spanish feelings toward Lutherans. The expedition leader was also required to take with him to Florida "one hundred horses, two hundred horned cattle, four hundred hogs, four hundred sheep and some goats, and five hundred slaves."[34] The African slaves were "to aid in cultivating the land and building" necessary structures.[35]

Additionally, the contract between Philip and Menéndez stipulated that 12 priests and four fathers of the Jesuit order would accompany the expedition. Menéndez was obligated to build two or three settlements, each for about 100 families. Each town was to have its own fort in order to defend itself from the French and Native Americans.

For his efforts, Menéndez received the title of *adelantado*, which was the equivalent of governor. The post also included military powers. The title comes from a Spanish phrase that means one who goes before. The role of the adelantado as leader of an expedition where no Spaniards had yet gone was therefore implied. The appointment to the position was a standard practice for explorers in the Americas. In addition, his rank as a member of the Spanish nobility was raised to marquis, which was a hereditary title to be passed on to his heirs. From the Florida province, Menéndez was allowed to claim a large piece of land for his own uses. Finally, Philip agreed to pay Menéndez a large annual salary. The new governor was also entitled to a percentage of all royal duties collected from Florida ports. To emphasize the importance of Menéndez and Florida within the Spanish Empire, Menéndez had "the freedom of all other ports of New Spain."[36]

Philip also included a less formal note to Menéndez in the final paperwork. The king "emphasized the need to convert the Indians to the holy Faith."[37] According to Philip, bringing Christianity to the natives "was the primary motive of the Crown in seeking to populate" Florida.[38] Menéndez took seriously the task of establishing friendly relations with the Native Americans. He understood that cultivating warm relationships would go a long way in helping the spread of Catholicism among the natives.

6

San Augustín

Pedro Menéndez de Avilés set sail from Cadiz, Spain, on July 1, 1565, with 11 ships holding about 2,600 men. Severe storms damaged some of the vessels, forcing them back to Europe. By the time the fleet reached New Spain, only about half of his force was intact. True to his nature, however, Menéndez did not hesitate. Immediately, he replenished his vessels and headed north to Florida. The founding of Spain's first permanent settlement in North America was less than a month away.

A TRUSTED FEW

Pedro Menéndez took several trustworthy individuals with him on his expedition. Each of these "were men who stood in close personal relationship with him, for they shared common bonds of blood or marriage."[39] Each man was a gentleman from Asturias with extensive sailing experience. Among these men were his brother Bartolomé, his nephew Pedro Menéndez Márquez, Esteban de las Alas, and Diego Flores Valdés. "All of these top-level lieutenants of Menéndez could count many years of command experience and were thus qualified to serve in the Florida expedition."[40]

Bartolomé "had served long and loyally with his brother" for many years.[41] Bartolomé was a capable commander and had endured prison with Pedro in 1563–64. Pedro Menéndez Márquez was a valuable resource for his uncle. Menéndez had served with him before, allowing Pedro Menéndez Márquez to command ships under him. While reporting to the Crown, Menéndez described Menéndez Márquez as "one of the most expert mariners" serving Spain.[42] Menéndez named his nephew second in command of the northern fleet. A kinsman of the Menéndez brothers, Esteban de las Alas was also a family friend from their hometown of Avilés. He married into the family in 1533. Like Bartolomé, Esteban had extensive experience as a commander and had suffered through some time in prison for political reasons. Menéndez trusted Esteban, placing him "in charge of the two northern elements of the Florida expedition."[43] Thus, Menéndez only needed to concern himself with the bulk of the group, which would focus their energies on establishing a colony in the south. Finally, Diego Flores Valdés was a career seaman who went into debt in order to serve his country at sea. Menéndez installed Diego Flores as second in command of the southern fleet. These were the men Menéndez most trusted as he made preparations for the expedition to Florida.

A NEW SETTLEMENT ON THE FLORIDA COAST

Menéndez arrived in Puerto Rico on August 9, 1565. There, he found out that the French ships headed to Florida had left before him. Without delay, Menéndez ordered the fleet to make its way north. Menéndez knew that French efforts to supply fresh provisions for their settlement were underway. Menéndez did not want to wait too long. He understood the French threatened his chances of success and he eagerly anticipated seeing Florida and establishing a Spanish presence there. He did not have long to wait.

On August 28, 1565, Menéndez first saw the Florida coastline. The date was significant to him, because it was celebrated on the Catholic calendar as St. Augustine's day (Augustine of Hippo was the patron saint of his hometown of Avilés). As Menéndez eyed the coast, he approached "a good harbor with a good beach."[44] He named the place *San Augustín*, Spanish for St. Augustine. The governor sailed north until he sighted the French colony and four French ships. He returned to the natural harbor and on September 8, Menéndez came ashore and formally christened the colony. It was a day of great celebration. First, the Spanish made a big show of coming ashore. Flag bearers led the way as trumpets announced the arrival of the new governor. Soldiers marched in step to the constant drumbeat. The Spanish ships let off cannon blast after cannon blast. Many of the local Native Americans watched as Menéndez stepped from his small boat and set foot on Florida soil. Waiting to meet him was Francisco Lopez de Mendoza Grajales, a Catholic priest. The cleric carried a cross and sang a religious song, *Te Deum Laudamus*, a Latin hymn of praise. According to church tradition, the hymn was partially written by Saint Augustine. It was common for priests to include the singing of *Te Deum* for such events. Menéndez fell to his knees and kissed the cross. Then, he immediately asked the priests to conduct a Mass.[45] After taking care of the religious requirements, Menéndez then proclaimed that Florida belonged to Spain. Finally, the rest of the day was devoted to a feast in celebration of the new Spanish colony.

LAYING FOUNDATIONS

Although the celebration might have seemed frivolous, there were important reasons why Menéndez went to such lengths. The ceremonies were "the first stage of a Spanish conquest."[46]

AUGUSTINE THE SAINT

Weighing anchor off the coast of Florida on August 28, 1565, Pedro Menéndez de Avilés saw the location of his new fort for the first time. The day happened to be one in which the Roman Catholic Church honored one of its most important early figures, Augustine of Hippo. Augustine's story is compelling.

Aurelius Augustine was born in A.D. 354 in North Africa. His mother was a devout Christian, but his father was a pagan. Augustine was bright, but for a time, he sought a life of pleasure. Discovering his life lacked meaning, Augustine converted to Christianity in A.D. 387, receiving the rite of baptism on Easter Sunday. The new convert went to Rome to study for a year. Then, he returned to Africa, where he established a monastic community, a religious group of people who voluntarily isolate themselves from the world and its influences. Augustine believed in the monastic lifestyle and shunned holding any church office. However, the needs of the Church finally coaxed him into serving as a priest in 391. Five years later, when Augustine was 42 years old, the Church appointed him bishop of Hippo.

Augustine wrote several important works that helped shape doctrine of the Catholic Church. These doctrinal matters included topics such as grace, sexuality, free will, and the soul. His writings include *Confessions*, *The City of God*, and *Exposition on the Psalms*. Many believe his *Confessions* to be the first autobiography ever written.

When the raiding Vandals (Germanic tribes) arrived in Africa, Augustine rejected the opportunity to leave the city and his congregation. The bishop emphatically declared his faith in God to save him and the city. The Vandals surrounded the city and laid siege to it. Three months into the siege, Augustine became ill with a fever. A short time later, the 76-year-old bishop died on August 28, 430. The Church later named August 28 the feast day for this saint from Africa. Such was the namesake of Pedro Menéndez's settlement in Florida—a settlement that has been continuously occupied since 1565.

That is to say, the establishment of political power there provided the basis for economic development and the way in which the colony would operate. Menéndez accomplished this by publicly taking possession of the land. In doing so, he "fulfilled

St. Augustine, Florida, was named in honor of St. Augustine of Hippo, an African bishop who was one of the most important figures in the development of Western Christianity.

The Great (or Long) House of the chief of the Seloy tribe of the Timucuan nation could hold 300 people.

The Spanish who arrived in 1565 were invited by the chief of the Seloy to occupy the Great House.

Moat dug by the Spanish. Some traces of such a moat have recently been excavated.

Shortly after their arrival at St. Augustine, the Spanish colonists were invited to live in the Great House of the chief of the Seloy tribe. The thatched structure was capable of holding several hundred people, and the Spanish quickly transformed it into a defensible position.

the requirements of the King's ordinances for conquest."[47] Now that the king's laws had been fulfilled, the conquest of Florida could begin.

In order to rule Florida effectively, Menéndez knew that St. Augustine must be protected. Immediately, he went about shoring up its defenses. Upon Menéndez's arrival, the local Native Americans honored the Spanish leader by presenting him with "a large mansion belonging to the chief, situated near the banks of the river."[48] The new residents had little to work with. One of the men remarked that "there is not a stone to be found in the whole country."[49] Lacking stone, Menéndez and his men worked with what was available. Without delay, the Spanish put up an earthen wall around the house. Then, they dug a ditch around the entire compound. To arm the fort, 80 cannon were brought from the ships, the smallest of which weighed 2,500 pounds. It may not have been impressive to look at, but Menéndez had transformed the site into a formidable defensive position. Menéndez knew the French would soon come, and the Spanish wanted to be ready for them.

To maintain law and order, Menéndez appointed judges and instituted a local court system, patterned after the Spanish local system. St. Augustine might have been on the frontier, but its citizens were expected to behave as if they lived in Spain.

During his time in Florida, Menéndez followed this same pattern each time he founded a settlement. First, he took care to observe all the expected religious ceremonies: acknowledging the priests, displaying the cross, and participating in a Mass. The religious rites were always followed by the secular formalities in which he took possession of the land in the name of the king of Spain. Then, Menéndez turned his eye to the short-term and long-term defense of the colony. This last step was an obvious need, especially with other countries such as France vying for influence in the region.

Menéndez founded the new settlement as an investment that would be profitable. The governor wanted to become "Florida's first great land developer, industrialist, and agribusinessman."[50] Despite his hard work, Menéndez never realized the hoped-for financial returns from his colony. There were many reasons for this lack of profit. First, the conditions were harsh, leading to frequent mutinies among his soldiers. Second, the land never yielded a major find of any valuable mineral, precious metal, or stones. Third, the governor's Indian policy depended almost solely upon him, resulting in a virtually constant state of warfare with the local natives. Fourth, many of the lesser officials administering the local government were corrupt. Finally, the land along the coast simply could not consistently produce a bounty of crops. Any one of these issues, if reversed, might have resulted in a profitable colony.

Despite its strategic location along the northeastern coast of what is today Florida, St. Augustine did not prove to be profitable for the Spanish. The region lacked valuable mineral resources and the land along the coast was too sandy to produce agricultural crops.

Instead, St. Augustine was forced to rely on the annual *situado,* or subsidy, from Spanish Mexico. This subsidy consisted of food, various supplies, and currency. The settlement's dependence upon outside support severely limited the ability of the colony to grow, throughout its existence. Even today, despite its prime location on the Florida coast, St. Augustine is just a small community numbering only about 12,000 people.

FORT CAROLINE

As the Spanish settled into St. Augustine, a French expedition was struggling to establish a settlement north of the Spanish colony. The French called their colony Fort Caroline. It had been established the year before, in 1564. Fort Caroline, named for the French king Charles IX, was situated very near the present-day border between Florida and Georgia, at present-day Jacksonville. The settlement sat on the banks of the River Mai (St. Johns River), giving it access to the Atlantic Ocean.

The colony had enjoyed early successes. Relations with the local Native Americans were good. The colonists quickly put up defensive walls and built crude houses. The settlement was composed of several hundred people, mostly soldiers. Soon, however, the lack of supplies led to bickering and conflict among the colonists. Sickness spread and began to take its toll. Admiral Jean Ribault decided to return to Europe to get supplies. Ribault left the colony in the hands of René de Laudonnière, a "handsome but unpopular aristocrat."[51] With Ribault gone, Laudonnière decided to make the most of a bad situation. Rather than wait patiently for Ribault and supplies to return from Europe, the headstrong commander decided to begin raiding Spanish ships en route to Europe. This proved to be the undoing of the colony. The Spanish believed that the French fort served only one purpose: to prey on unsuspecting Spanish ships filled with gold and silver from Mexico and Peru. Spain lodged protests with France. The French ignored their complaints. Realizing the French had no intention of respecting Spanish rights, "King Philip of Spain decided to take matters into his own hands."[52] He did so when he appointed Menéndez to lead the expedition to Florida. If France would not respect Spanish rights voluntarily, then France would have to deal with Pedro Menéndez.

7

Removing the French Threat

French admiral Jean Ribault returned to Fort Caroline just days before Menéndez arrived at St. Augustine. Ribault decided to act quickly and move against the Spanish force before they could establish themselves. The French leader took almost every available fighting man in good health and loaded them on one of several ships. Then, the French force headed south toward St. Augustine. As they headed toward the new settlement, Menéndez watched the approaching ships. However, the sky indicated that the weather was about to turn. The French fleet came close enough to St. Augustine that they threatened to attack the Spanish and seize their small settlement. But the weather prevented Ribault from completing his task. The winds began driving the French fleet south, farther and farther away from St. Augustine. Ribault and his men could do nothing against the wind. Helplessly, the French fleet watched as the Spanish settlement grew smaller and smaller in the distance. Now, Ribault had other things to worry about—namely, successfully riding out the storm.

Meanwhile, Menéndez watched the winds and rain. He had seen this kind of storm before. He knew that the storm was not a small squall that would quickly blow over. Instead, this was a large tropical storm, probably a hurricane. With the fierce storm driving the French fleet southward, Menéndez recognized that an opportunity existed to damage the enemy force at Fort Caroline. He knew that if he were Ribault, he would have almost emptied the fort in order to have as large an attack force as possible. It might be several days before the French ships filled with soldiers could sail back north to their fort. Until then, the fort was probably in a weak position.

A BOLD PLAN

Menéndez realized that the French fort located north of St. Augustine was now vulnerable. Calling together his advisors, the governor revealed a daring plan to travel by land during the storm and attack the French at Fort Caroline. His advisors opposed the idea, but Menéndez overruled them. On September 17, Menéndez led more than 500 men out of the safety of the fort and into the rains of a Florida hurricane.

It was a bold move. But Menéndez was a sailor and knew that the winds would delay the return of Ribault and his men. Menéndez also guessed that the French leader had depleted the defenses of his fort in his failed attempt to attack St. Augustine. Thus, the bulk of Ribault's forces were no longer at Fort Caroline. Instead, they faced the onslaught of a hurricane.

Menéndez and his men marched in the pouring rain. Their guides were two Indian chiefs who had been offended by the French. As they made their way north, natural barriers stood between them and their prize. Heavy rains turned the small streams and shallow marshes into raging rivers and large lakes. At times, the men were forced to wade through water up to their necks, holding their weapons above their heads. The men were miserable. "Many of the officers and men wished to return" to St. Augustine.[53] The group continued on, in large part due to the unrelenting drive of their leader. Menéndez refused to give up, knowing that such an opportunity to destroy the French might never again present itself.

THE HARQUEBUS

The harquebus (sometimes spelled arquebus) was the primary firearm of the Spanish during the sixteenth century. A primitive weapon, the harquebus was a smoothbore, low-velocity firearm. Lighter in weight and smaller than earlier muskets, it was carried into battle with little difficulty. Sometimes, soldiers mounted larger, heavier versions of the weapon onto wagons for use in combat. Because most of these weapons, large and small, were crafted by blacksmiths, there were many variations on the basic design.

Essentially, the weapon was useless against good steel-plate armor. To the American natives, the harquebus was a visible sign of Spanish power. But Florida Indians quickly realized the limitations of the weapons. In order to use the firearm, a soldier placed a bullet, usually a ball, into the barrel. After that, he used a stick or ramrod to ram the bullet all the way down the barrel. The soldier then used a forked pole to steady the end of the barrel. Thus, the intended target was alerted to the threat. To fire the harquebus, the soldier then lowered a piece of burning fuse into the barrel. Then, he waited for the fuse to set fire to the packed charge in the barrel. The process was slow and laborious. Worse still, the weapons often misfired, failing to fire correctly. "Thus, these weapons had the disadvantages of a lengthy loading and firing process as well as" being unpredictable—especially in combat.* Florida Indians often timed their attacks so that they exposed themselves only while the Spaniards reloaded or while they waited for the fuse to ignite the charge. The weapons also relied on dry gunpowder, which was sometimes difficult to maintain in the Florida climate.

Pedro Menéndez and his men used the harquebus when they attacked the French at Fort Caroline. However, by the end of the sixteenth century, the increased use of higher-velocity muskets began to replace the harquebus. Use of the weapon soon diminished.

---

* Shane Mountjoy, *Francisco Pizarro and the Conquest of the Inca* (Philadelphia, Pa.: Chelsea House Publishers, 2005), 31.

THE FRENCH FORT

Meanwhile, the French in Fort Caroline faced their own difficulties. The fort suffered from a "lack of vigorous leadership,"[54] because authority was divided between two leaders, the Sieur de Lys and René de Laudonnière. Many within the fort were suffering from illness. In addition, the more decisive of the two coleaders, René de Laudonnière, was one of those who was ill. By the time the Spanish arrived, there were only "sixteen or seventeen well men in the fort."[55] Worse still, Ribault had stripped the settlement of virtually every able-bodied soldier. He had left some behind, but some of these "had never drawn a sword—four being boys who kept Ribau[l]t's dogs; one cook; a carpenter," and several others unfit to fight in battle.[56] In total, Ribault left about 85 people, including women and children, under the care of Laudonnière.

The French commander feared a possible attack, especially when Ribault failed to return, and the storm began unleashing its vengeance on the fort. Laudonnière appointed two captains to stand watch; to ensure readiness in case of attack. Unfortunately for the French, the storm allowed them to relax. "The night of September 19 was very stormy" and the captain of the watch believed it impossible for anyone to be out in such weather.[57] At daybreak, the officer on duty sent all but one of the guards to bed and then went to his quarters.

THE END OF FORT CAROLINE

At almost the exact time the first line of Fort Caroline's defenses were leaving their posts, Menéndez and his men arrived at the French fort. The Spanish men were weary from marching three days in the rain. But Menéndez knew that they might be discovered if they delayed. The attack began soon after they arrived. The Spaniards captured the single French sentry still

In 1564, French Huguenot explorer René de Laudonnière led a 300-man expedition to establish a settlement at the mouth of what is today St. Johns River, near present-day Jacksonville, Florida. Laudonnière named the settlement Fort Caroline in honor of King Charles IX of France.

standing guard outside the walls. He cried out, which should have alerted the men inside. Instead, those guarding the gate became confused and opened it. Spanish attackers poured through the open gate.

The battle did not last long. French soldiers rushed out to meet the attackers. Many of the defenders were "in their nightclothing."[58] The Spaniards quickly overran the defenses, killing 132 of the defenders. One historian claims that it "must have been a confused, violent scene."[59] One French survivor later said, "They made a pretty butchery of it."[60] Women and children were spared. With the fort lost, 45 scaled the wall and either escaped into the woods or swam to the French ships anchored nearby.

Spanish accounts reveal that some of the French captives were killed after surrendering. Menéndez ordered that no harm should come to any woman, child, or boy under the age of 15. Shocking as it may be, "the rest were killed."[61] Spanish motives for the bloodshed were apparent: "Some of the prisoners were hung" from trees.[62] Above their heads, an inscription in Spanish declared the reason for the executions—"Not as Frenchmen, but as Lutherans."[63] This battle was not so much a conflict between two rival European states as it was a clash between two competing views of Christianity. The fall of Fort Caroline was simply the first in a series of battles between the two opponents.

Menéndez made sure the fort was securely in his control, and then opened negotiations with Jacques Ribault, the French commander's son who was safely on board one of the nearby ships. The two sides talked for a while, but the younger Ribault did not seem to appreciate the reality of the situation. Menéndez decided to convey his message by firing on one of the smaller ships. Within minutes, the French ship was sunk. The remaining two French ships "cut their cables and moved closer

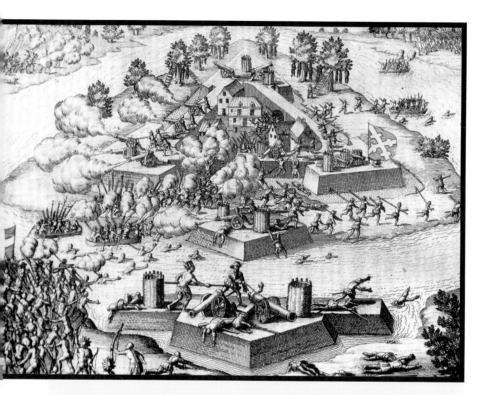

This engraving of the massacre at Fort Caroline depicts the Spanish attack, led by Pedro Menéndez de Avilés, on the 200-person French garrison in September 1565. With the exception of about 50 women and children and a few others who escaped, the majority of the fort's inhabitants were killed by Menéndez's forces.

to the river mouth, to comparative safety."[64] Menéndez now had full control of Fort Caroline and the River Mai.

The Spaniards celebrated their victory over the French. However, they soon found some items that deeply disturbed them: Lutheran books and other religious articles. To the Catholic victors, these items were sacrilegious and had to be destroyed. Menéndez ordered the offensive books burned. He kept a few of the other artifacts as proof that the fort had fallen. Also troubling to the soldiers were the female and children prisoners. To pacify his men, "Menéndez prepared to send the French dependents away as soon as possible."[65]

Menéndez also did what he could to make the fort defensible should the French fleet return. The fort's new owners repaired the walls and added to the fortifications. Menéndez "had crosses erected in prominent" locations and chose the site of a new church.[66] Laudonnière had a store of timber that he had intended to use for building ships. Ironically, Menéndez ordered the wood be used to construct a Catholic church. Finally, because the day before the Spanish captured the fort was St. Matthew's Day, he renamed the fort San Mateo (St. Matthew) as a tribute to the apostle. The river was also renamed, from Mai to San Mateo.

Leaving the bulk of his men, Menéndez returned to St. Augustine. The creeks and swamps were even more difficult to cross than they had been just a few days earlier. After much difficulty, the governor and his small band of soldiers arrived to "great rejoicings."[67] As was his custom, Menéndez first celebrated Mass and gave thanks for the great victory. Then, he and the others celebrated their triumph over the French Lutherans.

A LINE IN THE SAND

Following the capture of the French fort, Menéndez felt their chances of defeating the French had improved, but he did not relax. He knew that Ribault and his men might still return and challenge the Spanish presence at St. Augustine. He waited anxiously for any sign of the French ships.

Then, a week after returning to St. Augustine, Menéndez learned from local Native Americans that a group of Frenchmen were about 18 miles south of his colony. The governor took 50 men with him to deal with them. After negotiating with Menéndez, the French surrendered to him. However,

Shortly after the massacre at Fort Caroline, the Spanish effectively ended France's attempt at colonizing Florida by killing Jean Ribault and the majority of his 150-man force. Despite being forced from Florida, the French would gain a measure of revenge when a French force led by Dominic de Gourgues killed the inhabitants of Fort San Mateo (the former Fort Caroline) in 1568.

"Menéndez, who had neither guards nor provisions" for so many prisoners, killed them on the beach.[68]

The slaughter was appalling, but somewhat understandable. The fledgling settlement lacked the necessary supplies for its own members, let alone for a large group of prisoners. The religious differences may have helped Menéndez ease his conscience.

Less than two weeks later, he received word that another and larger group of men was now at the same inlet about 18 miles south of St. Augustine. This time, Menéndez took a larger force with him, about 150 soldiers. Now, Ribault himself was in the group trying to cross the inlet. As before, Menéndez informed the French that he had captured Fort Caroline. Also as before, the two sides engaged in discussions concerning the terms of surrender. Once again, Menéndez refused to make any promises other than the prisoners would be at his mercy.

Ribault and his officers took a night to think it over. Two hundred of his men refused to surrender, choosing instead to face whatever dangers might lie in the interior. They fled during the night. The remaining 150 were ferried across the inlet in groups of 10 aboard a Spanish boat. There, they were fed and then had their hands bound behind them. The French commander, sensing what lay in store, reportedly said, "From earth we came, and to the earth we must return; that twenty years of life, more or less, did not matter."[69] Ribault bravely walked to the same line where others under his command had died just two weeks earlier. The Spanish again killed helpless Frenchmen as they marched up the beach. To commemorate what happened there, the place is still called *Matanzas*, "the place of the slaughter."

8

Securing
the Colony

In spite of the bloodshed Pedro Menéndez inflicted on his
French rivals, his relationship with the Florida tribes was one
of friendship. His talent for forming friendships with the Native Americans was unrivalled among other Spanish explorers.
Indeed, the story of most Spanish explorers' treatment of the
tribes is one of deceit, mistreatment, and bloodshed. St. Augustine continued to face hardships and the threat of hostile
takeover, sometimes even from natives. But the leadership of
Menéndez ensured that the greatest threats to the colony were
not from local Native Americans, but from other Europeans.
He made efforts to forge lasting relationships of peace with the
tribes he encountered.

CHIEF CARLOS
Now that France no longer threatened St. Augustine, Pedro
Menéndez decided to explore some of the surrounding areas.
He also hoped to establish friendly relations with the Native
Americans, thereby increasing the colony's chances of survival.

Despite having difficulties with the French, Pedro Menéndez fostered a peaceful relationship with Florida's Indian tribes. Depicted here is a Florida Indian chief from the sixteenth century.

Menéndez departed the new settlement and explored the Florida Keys, as well as parts of southwestern Florida.

While exploring this region, Menéndez discovered that a local Indian chief named Carlos held some Spaniards captive. In order to free his countrymen, the governor deceived Carlos. First, Menéndez invited Carlos and several of his advisors to his ship. There, after exchanging gifts, the Native Americans and Spaniards all ate a large meal. Then, Carlos announced he was ready to leave. Menéndez explained that Carlos held some Spaniards, and now was the time to release them. Carlos offered to go get the men himself, but the governor merely smiled and shook his head. Menéndez was not going to allow Carlos to escape. Instead, he knew that holding the chief offered the best chance of freeing the captives.

Carlos considered trying to escape, but Menéndez had placed soldiers along the edge of the ship to prevent such an attempt. Also, there were soldiers well placed among Carlos's people. For Carlos, the only way to freedom was to give up the Spanish prisoners. Recognizing his limited options, Carlos agreed to send some of his men to get the Spanish prisoners. The men went back to shore and quickly returned with the remaining eight survivors of the shipwreck. True to his belief in fostering good relations, Menéndez later visited Carlos to make sure their friendship was intact. Carlos welcomed the governor into his home, and the two shared a great feast together.

BACK TO ST. AUGUSTINE

After spending some time exploring the Florida Keys and southwestern Florida, Menéndez returned to St. Augustine. He had a bold vision of what he wanted to accomplish next. The governor believed that St. Augustine could be used as a base from which more colonies could be set up to the north. Menéndez was excited to reach St. Augustine again and share his ideas for expanding Spanish growth in Florida. He made his way to the settlement he had founded the previous fall with a large contingent of men.

Arriving there on March 20, 1566, the governor found the St. Augustine colonists discouraged and on the verge of giving up. The settlers had endured a challenging winter. About 100 of the colonists had died, in large part due to a lack of adequate

THE UNWANTED GIFT

Not long after Chief Carlos released the Spanish prisoners, Pedro Menéndez paid him a visit in his village. Carlos lived in an immense home. Spanish accounts note that the dwelling could hold 2,000 people. Even if the descriptions are somewhat exaggerated, Carlos was a wealthy man who lived in a large house.

Even though Menéndez had earlier used the threat of force to free the Spanish captives, Carlos was pleased to see the governor. The chief warmly welcomed his Spanish friends. Menéndez delighted the natives when he spoke to them in their own language! The two leaders sat together, exchanged gifts, and ate and drank together. While they sat together, Carlos brought out a beautiful young woman to sit with them. Menéndez assumed the woman was Carlos's wife. The three enjoyed themselves as the festivities continued.

Then, Carlos revealed that he had a gift of great importance to present to Menéndez. The governor listened attentively as Carlos explained that the woman sitting with them was not his wife, but his sister. Next, the Spanish leader strained to make sure he heard Carlos correctly. The interpreter translated the last few words to Menéndez. Carlos was giving his sister to Menéndez for a wife!

The governor was stunned. He already had a wife, Ana María, back in Spain. Under Roman Catholic beliefs, Menéndez could not marry more than one woman, but he did not want to offend Carlos. St. Augustine's founder decided to sidestep the issue. He thanked Carlos for his generous gift. Then, he took his new wife back to his ship. There, he placed her in the care of the Spanish women on board. They baptized Carlos's sister and gave her the name Antonia. Later, Antonia boarded another ship in the fleet and went to Havana. There, she received religious teachings consistent with the Catholic faith. Menéndez never married the Native American woman given to him as a gift.

food and medicine. Another 100 had given up, moving to the Caribbean. Menéndez left supplies and about 150 men at St. Augustine. He stopped briefly at San Mateo, leaving another 150 of his men as reinforcements for the fort there. Then, the expedition sailed north until it arrived at a natural harbor off the coast of modern-day Georgia.

THE MIRACLE OF RAIN

Local Native Americans greeted them on the shore near the place they called Guale. At first, the natives were distrustful of the strangers. Menéndez, however, quickly won them over with his gifts of food and displays of friendship. A Frenchman living with the Native Americans, the survivor of a shipwreck, served as a translator. In conversation, Menéndez discovered that the natives in Guale held two Indian prisoners from Orista, a place nearby. The people in Guale were in the midst of a drought that had lasted many months. Their crops had failed, and the natives faced starvation. The Guales believed that some great sacrifice must be made in order to end the drought. In order to appease the rain gods, the Guales intended to sacrifice the two prisoners.

The situation shocked Menéndez. He decided to intervene. He requested custody of the Orista captives. He promised that he would end the war between the two regions if he could take the two prisoners to Orista as a sign of friendship. The governor also mentioned that the lack of rain was not due to the need for human sacrifices, but rather the penalty from God because of the plans to sacrifice the humans. The Guales were hesitant, but permitted Menéndez to take the two captives after the Spaniard agreed to leave some of his men in place of the prisoners.

Menéndez took the two prisoners home to the Orista Indians. He offered the natives peace, which they accepted. After meeting with them, Menéndez returned to Guale, sharing the news of peace with the Oristas. The Guales were delighted that hostilities were over. And then something remarkable occurred. It rained. The region of Guale received a heavy shower of rain. Amazingly, the rain only fell on Guale lands. Of course, the natives attributed the rain to Menéndez. Word quickly spread throughout the region of the incredible downpour and the governor's unique bond with the god of rain.

As a result of this incident, Menéndez was a welcome visitor to virtually all villages in the region. The Spaniard followed a regular practice in which he landed on the beach, went into the village, and met with the natives. Often, he brought gifts for the villagers. Then, with the permission of the local leaders, he would set up a wooden cross in the village. This cross served as a reminder to the Native Americans that Menéndez was a faithful Christian. The Native Americans probably believed that the cross also might bring them rain or some other good fortune.

After visiting Indian tribes throughout the region, Pedro Menéndez returned to St. Augustine in August 1566. Again, he did not stay long. This time, he was there long enough to squelch another revolt. He laid down the law, forcing the colonists to endure their hardships. Notably, he issued "seventeen ordinances for the governing of Florida."[70] These so-called *Ordinances of Government* were the first European set of laws instituted in North America. After reinforcing St. Augustine, Menéndez then headed south to the Caribbean Sea in order to fulfill another obligation of his position, something he was perfectly suited to do: fighting pirates.

MENÉNDEZ REPORTS TO THE KING

Menéndez returned to the Caribbean, but found no pirates to fight. Reports of pirate ships proved only to be rumors. After amassing almost 1,000 fighting men and eight ships, the governor of Florida had little to do. Hearing further rumors

Shortly after he returned to Spain in 1567, Pedro Menéndez met with King Philip II (depicted here) and informed the king of his success in driving the French from Florida. In recognition of his accomplishments in Florida, King Philip appointed Menéndez captain general of Spain's West Indian treasure fleet.

of a large French fleet in the region, he reinforced Spanish forts on Puerto Rico, Hispaniola, and Cuba. He waited for a short time, then grew impatient with the lack of activity.

Once more, Menéndez went to Florida. This time, he helped put down Indian revolts, tried to improve relations with the Native Americans, visited each of the Spanish settlements, and provided provisions for the colonists.

Still, Pedro Menéndez was restless. He had been away from Spain for a long time. He felt the need to return home and give an account of his expedition to King Philip. So, in May 1567, he sailed to Spain. After a monthlong voyage, his ship reached Spanish waters. As soon as Menéndez landed, he immediately made his way to the church. There, he got down on his knees and offered a prayer of thanksgiving for his safe journey. He received Mass; then, he proceeded home, followed by many of the local townspeople. After seeing his wife and family, Menéndez went to Madrid to see the king.

Menéndez gave his report to King Philip. He described the encounters with the French, including how he had killed the "non-believing" Frenchmen. Philip gave Menéndez his full attention. The more he heard, the more he was impressed. Menéndez had achieved even more than the king had hoped. To show his appreciation, Philip appointed Menéndez captain general of the West, a new position. While in Spain, he also received many high honors. It seemed as though things were finally going well for Menéndez. Soon, however, news from the New World raised new concerns for the captain general of the West.

9

A Coveted Place

Pedro Menéndez was in Spain, enjoying a well-deserved rest from his duties in the New World. He accepted honors for his exploits in Florida. All seemed well, but then disturbing news from Florida began to trickle in. The Florida Indians had revolted and had completely wiped out one Spanish settlement. And most troubling was the report that a French force had destroyed San Mateo. Menéndez worried that his enterprise in Florida was about to fall apart. Quickly, he gathered the necessary supplies and men and headed back to the New World.

THE FRENCH GET REVENGE

Menéndez rushed back to Florida, but for those at San Mateo, it was too late. A French force led by Dominic de Gourgues had already decimated the fort. De Gourgues had reason to hate the Spanish. Captured by Spain some years before, de Gourgues was spared, but forced to serve aboard a Spanish galley as an oarsman. It was a miserable existence. Later, the French captured the Spanish ship, and he gained his liberty. Once freed, the Frenchman vowed to make the Spanish pay for his mistreatment. De Gourgues made his way to Florida and set his sights on San Mateo. Allied with local Native Americans whom the Spaniards had mistreated, the French-led force had overrun the fort's defenses.

After the battle, some of the Spanish captives were led out to the very spot where Menéndez had hanged French captives when he had captured the fort in 1565. De Gourgues recounted what he believed to be the crimes committed by the Spanish: killing French subjects; seizing French forts; and occupying Florida. Such behavior demanded punishment. De Gourgues indicated he wished to torture them, but instead chose to simply execute them. He then ordered them hanged from the same oak trees Menéndez had hanged the Huguenots from two years earlier. Then, he wrote his own version of the earlier Spanish inscription ("Not as Frenchmen, but as Lutherans"[71]): "I do this, not as to Spaniards, nor as to outcasts, but as to traitors, thieves, and murderers."[72] The words were "engraved, on a tablet of pine, with a red-hot iron."[73]

After the grisly deed was done, de Gourgues convened a meeting with the Native Americans. He reminded them of his promise to rid them of the Spaniards. Then he encouraged the natives to do what they wanted to the fort. The Native Americans tore down the walls and burned anything of value. San Mateo was completely destroyed.

MENÉNDEZ TRAVELS A GREAT DEAL

Pedro Menéndez arrived in Florida shortly after de Gourgues left. Only then did Menéndez learn of the devastating attack on San Mateo. Worse yet, the Native Americans around St. Augustine were emboldened to defiantly show their hostility to the Spaniards there. Menéndez did all he could to soothe tensions. He especially focused on mission efforts to the Native Americans, much as he had in the past.

The conditions in Florida demanded the presence of Menéndez. It seemed as if he alone had the leadership necessary to keep the peace and develop the colony. But it was not to be. By early fall 1569, St. Augustine's founder was again in Spain. His position as captain general of the West forced him to travel to and from Florida again in 1570 and in 1571. Such a pace was grueling. Yet, the adelantado continued to do all he could for Florida, while still performing his other duties. His final trip to Florida began in May 1571. This time, Menéndez faced still more challenges.

SHIPWRECKED

By the time he reached St. Augustine, it was already December 1571. Storm season was now upon him. Menéndez made the stay as brief as possible. Supplies and reinforcements were unloaded. The governor shared his optimism with the colonists, and then turned his eyes southward. Although it was risky, Menéndez left for Havana on December 20, 1571. His "fleet" was composed of just three small ships. He was on one of the small ones, which held only 30 men. They sailed south toward the Caribbean when disaster struck. A storm drove them onto the beach, about 30 leagues (168 kilometers) south of St. Augustine, much as Ribault had been six years earlier.

As they stood huddled on the beach riding out the tropical storm, one wonders if Menéndez thought of the French in almost the same place six years earlier. When the storm subsided, Menéndez judged the damage done to the ship to be irreparable. From the wreckage, they hastily constructed a fort for defense. Amazingly, their harquebuses made it to shore unharmed. They even managed to preserve a fair amount of dry powder.

No sooner had they completed their defenses than they were attacked by local Native Americans, "who gathered like wolves" to feed upon the seemingly helpless Spaniards.[74] Menéndez and his men fought them off. Then, under the cover of darkness, they headed north. Either by luck or good fortune, they found canoes near each inlet they needed to cross. When the Native Americans attacked, the Spanish refused to give in. In the end, every man managed to make it safely to St. Augustine.

The weary detachment had little time to rejoice. Within days of their arrival, an English fleet appeared off the coast and attacked the colony. Menéndez and his 30 men helped bolster the defenses. The English were convinced the fort's residents were committed to withstanding the assault and left. Once again, Menéndez had saved St. Augustine.

THE END OF AN ERA

In the spring of 1572, Pedro Menéndez returned to Spain. He would never again set foot in Florida. Instead, he sent supplies, colonists, and priests to the New World from Spain. After arriving in Spain, he began assembling a massive fleet, the largest yet for Spain. He spent the next two years collecting the ships, supplies, and men. King Philip named Menéndez captain general of the large fleet on February 10, 1574. It was his last great honor.

For future explorers, the Spanish world was about to change. Shortly before Menéndez died, Philip proclaimed changes to the Spanish system of colonization. These changes specified that the leader of any expedition could not make certain decisions by himself. Instead, the beliefs and principles of the Roman Catholic Church would act as the guiding force in any future expeditions. If Menéndez had lived longer, the new rules would have prevented him from doing all he had already done in Florida. The year 1574 marked the end of one era and the beginning of another in Spanish exploration.

To the end, Menéndez loved Florida. A week and a half before his death, he wrote, "After the salvation of my soul, there is nothing in this world I want more than to be in Florida."[75] Within days, the explorer lay sick in bed, suffering from a severe fever. At 55, he had been at sea for most of his life. King Philip II of Spain personally knew him. Menéndez had served his monarch faithfully for 20 years, since he had escorted Prince Philip to England for his marriage. Fever exhausted the explorer. As he had so many times in the past, Menéndez focused on what needed to be done. In the final days, he received communion and wrote his will. He died on September 17, 1574. And yet, his settlement of St. Augustine lived on. In spite of the odds against it, the colony survived. Today, it is the oldest continuously occupied European-established city in the United States.

ST. AUGUSTINE AFTER MENÉNDEZ

Following the death of Pedro Menéndez, the governorship of Florida was given to a string of individuals. Probably the most capable was a nephew of Menéndez, Pedro Menéndez Márquez, appointed governor in 1576. The colony continued to struggle, but the undying commitment to maintaining a presence at St. Augustine was quite evident. For example, Sir Francis Drake, an English privateer, attacked and destroyed much of the city in 1586. The wooden fort and a large portion of the city were burned. However, the residents and soldiers living there had safely fled to the surrounding woods. They simply waited for Drake and his men to leave. Then, they returned and began the process of rebuilding the city and fort.

With Menéndez dead, Spain no longer viewed Florida as a prized possession. The region never produced the kind of riches that poured forth from Mexico and Peru. Instead, the colony seemed to gobble up all the men and resources sent there. Spain continued to maintain a military presence in Florida, especially at St. Augustine, even building a fort there, the Castillo de San Marcos in the last quarter of the seventeenth century. But Florida's usefulness to Spain was limited. The colony was not profitable, but instead was a stronghold

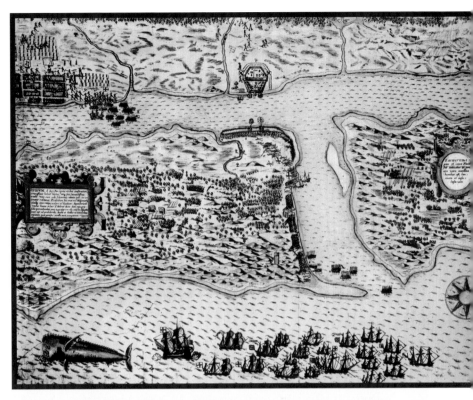

In 1586, English admiral Sir Francis Drake attacked and burned St. Augustine, forcing its residents to flee into the nearby woods. The attack is depicted in this engraving, the first of its kind for a U.S. city.

that served to keep the English colonies from encroaching on Spanish territories in the Caribbean.

A 21-YEAR OCCUPATION

After failing twice to capture St. Augustine and Castillo de San Marcos by force, the British finally acquired the city and fort in July 1763. They did so under the terms of the Treaty of Paris of 1763, which ended the Seven Years' War (called the French and Indian War in the American colonies). Britain had captured

Cuba and the Philippines, colonies of Spain, an ally of France and enemy of Britain during the conflict. Britain agreed to return these prize possessions in exchange for Florida. The fort was renamed St. Mark, which is the English form of San Marcos.

CASTILLO DE SAN MARCOS

Pedro Menéndez established St. Augustine in 1565. During the century following its founding, colonists built nine different wooden forts to protect the settlement. In 1672, the queen of Spain, Mariana, concluded that St. Augustine needed a stronger fort to provide security for the colony, especially against British colonialism. The result was Castillo de San Marcos. Workers quarried a unique stone to build the fort. Its walls are made of *coquina*, Spanish for little shells. The yellow stone is similar to limestone, formed from compacted layers of shells. Stone for the walls was quarried from Anastasia Island, located across the bay from the fort. Then, a kind of paste was prepared from crushed oyster shells, drying like cement. It took 23 years to complete the new stone fort, which still stands today.

The coquina walls of Castillo de San Marcos helped defend St. Augustine for nearly 150 years. The walls exhibited a rather unique characteristic: Cannon balls either harmlessly bounced off the walls or were absorbed. This quality became evident when the British attacked the fort in 1702. Despite a heavy bombardment, the walls remained virtually undamaged. The walls held, and the British attack failed.

After gaining control of the fort in 1821, the United States gave the Castillo the name Fort Marion. Few changes were made, but some of the storerooms were converted to prison cells. Osceola, the famed Seminole chief, was detained there in 1837.

After Florida seceded from the Union in December 1860, Union troops abandoned the fort, except for a lone caretaker. In January 1861, Southern troops marched on the fort, demanding that the man surrender. The single soldier refused to give up the fort without a written order. The Confederate forces complied, and the fort fell with no bloodshed. The Union retook the fort in March 1862, when the Union Navy received the surrender of the fort

During the American Revolution, Spain eventually allied itself with the United States against Britain. After the war ended, the Treaty of Paris of 1783 returned control of Florida, including the fort and city, to Spain. Spanish troops reclaimed the fort in July 1784, almost exactly 21 years after giving it up to the British.

and city without firing a shot. Throughout the rest of the nineteenth century, the fort housed Indian prisoners, as well as deserters from the Spanish-American War in 1898.

In 1900, the military moved the fort to inactive status, ending more than 200 years of service as a military fortification. In 1924, the U.S. government designated the fort a National Monument. Eighteen years later, the government restored its original name, the Castillo de San Marcos. Today, the old Spanish fort is a popular destination for tourists in St. Augustine.

Today a national monument, Castillo de San Marcos is the oldest masonry fort in the United States and is a popular tourist destination in St. Augustine.

INTO AMERICAN HANDS

Spain held Florida until 1821. As the United States continued to grow, conflicts began to arise between American forces and Florida Indians, especially the Seminoles. After years of aggravation, President James Monroe proposed to purchase Florida from Spain. The idea did not lack critics. John Randolph, a member of the U.S. House of Representatives, declared, "Florida, sir, is not worth buying, It is a land of swamps, of quagmires, of frogs, and alligators and mosquitoes! A man, sir, would not immigrate into Florida. No, sir! No man would immigrate into Florida—no, not from hell itself!"[76] Although he exaggerated the conditions of Florida, Randolph could not have foreseen the increased population of the state. Monroe had his way, and the United States received Florida, and St. Augustine, under the terms of the Adams-Onís Treaty, signed in 1819. The Americans formally took control of St. Augustine in July 1821. The colony of Pedro Menéndez de Avilés now lay in the hands of the United States of America. Twenty-four years later, in 1845, Florida became a state. The colonial period for St. Augustine and Florida had come to an end.

ST. AUGUSTINE TODAY

Today, St. Augustine, Florida, is a city of about 12,000 people. The city boasts a variety of cultural tastes, reflective of Indian, Spanish, British, and American influences. St. Augustine contains many buildings as examples of the Spanish Colonial Revival Style. As such, the community is a popular tourist destination. The city founded by Pedro Menéndez de Avilés continues today. Its survival is a testament to the spirit upon which it was founded more than 440 years ago, and to the man who founded it: Pedro Menéndez.

Chronology

1492 Ferdinand and Isabella drive the last of the Muslims, or Moors, from Spain; Christopher Columbus, a native of Genoa, sailing for Spain, "discovers" the New World.

1506 Christopher Columbus dies.

1513 *April 2* Juan Ponce de León lands in Florida, the first European to do so; Vasco de Nuñez de Balboa travels across the Isthmus of Panama, becoming the first European to see the Pacific Ocean.

1519 Pedro Menéndez is born in Avilés, Spain.

1521 Ponce de León returns to Florida's Gulf Coast to establish a colony but is killed by local natives.

1528 Pánfilo de Narváez begins his ill-fated mission to establish a settlement in Florida.

1531 Francisco Pizarro commences his expedition to conquer the Inca Empire of Peru.

1539 Hernando de Soto arrives in Florida, searching for gold; he eventually travels north and west, "discovering" the Mississippi River in 1542.

1540 Francisco Coronado begins his expedition into the American Southwest; he searches for the fabled Seven Cities of Gold, in part from information given to him by survivors of the Narváez expedition.

1561 King Philip II of Spain decides against making more attempts to colonize Florida.

1564 French Lutherans, led by Jean Ribault, land in northern Florida, and build Fort Caroline.

1565 *March 20* Philip II reverses policy and gives Pedro Menéndez de Avilés permission to settle Florida;

September 8 Pedro Menéndez establishes the colony of St. Augustine;

September 20 Menéndez and 500 of his men capture the French fort Caroline.

1566 Menéndez issues the *Ordinances of Government,* the first European laws instituted in North America; Spanish rebuild St. Augustine on Anastasia Island.

1572 The Spanish move St. Augustine back to the mainland.

1574 Pedro Menéndez, the founder of St. Augustine, dies.

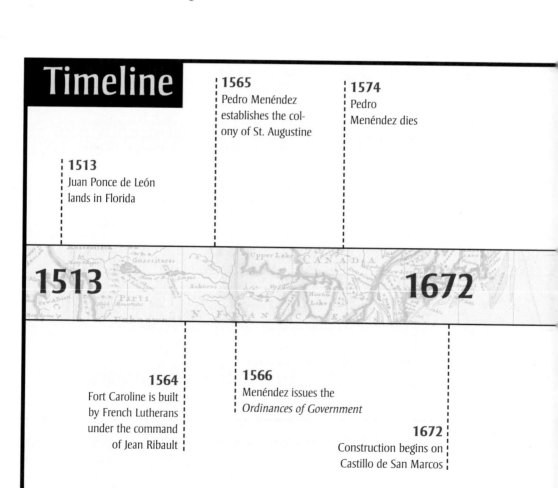

Timeline

1565
Pedro Menéndez establishes the colony of St. Augustine

1574
Pedro Menéndez dies

1513
Juan Ponce de León lands in Florida

1513

1672

1564
Fort Caroline is built by French Lutherans under the command of Jean Ribault

1566
Menéndez issues the *Ordinances of Government*

1672
Construction begins on Castillo de San Marcos

1586 English captain Sir Francis Drake attacks and burns St. Augustine; Spanish residents quickly rebuild the city.

1599 St. Augustine is destroyed by fires and flooding; again, the city is rebuilt.

1607 The English establish their first permanent North American settlement at Jamestown.

1672 Construction begins on Castillo de San Marcos.

1695 Castillo de San Marcos is completed.

1763 Spain loses control of Florida to Great Britain.

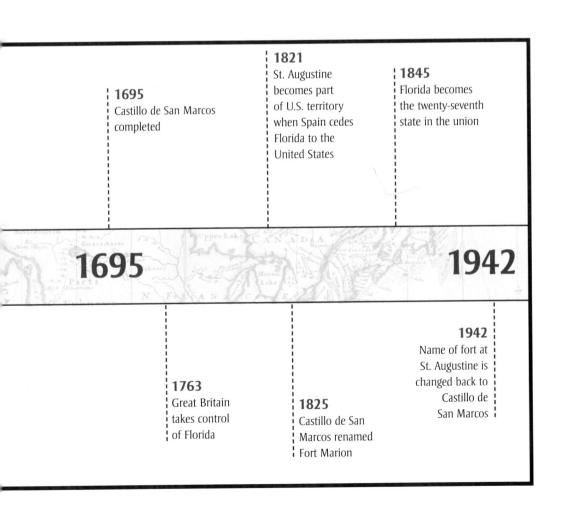

1695
Castillo de San Marcos completed

1821
St. Augustine becomes part of U.S. territory when Spain cedes Florida to the United States

1845
Florida becomes the twenty-seventh state in the union

1695

1942

1763
Great Britain takes control of Florida

1825
Castillo de San Marcos renamed Fort Marion

1942
Name of fort at St. Augustine is changed back to Castillo de San Marcos

1783 The American Revolution ends and Britain
returns control of Florida to Spain.

1819 Spain cedes Florida to the United States under
the terms of the Adams-Onís Treaty.

1821 St. Augustine becomes part of U.S. territory
when Spain officially turns over control of Florida
to the United States.

1825 Castillo de San Marcos is renamed Fort Marion
by the United States.

1845 Florida becomes the twenty-seventh state in
the union.

1942 The name of St. Augustine's fort is changed back
to Castillo de San Marcos.

Notes

Chapter 1

1. George R. Fairbanks, *The History and Antiquities of the City of St. Augustine, Florida* (reprint of the 1858 edition) (Gainesville: University Press of Florida, 1975), 68.
2. Ibid.
3. Ibid.
4. George Fairbanks, *History of Florida: From its Discovery by Ponce de León, in 1512, to the Close of the Florida War, in 1842* (Philadelphia: J.B. Lippincott & Co., 1871), 122.
5. Ibid.
6. Ibid.
7. Ibid., 123.
8. Fairbanks, *History of Florida*, 123.

Chapter 2

9. Shane Mountjoy, *Francisco Coronado and the Seven Cities of Gold* (Philadelphia: Chelsea House Publishers, 2005), 27.

Chapter 3

10. Fairbanks, *History of Florida*, 13.
11. Robert H. Fuson, *Juan Ponce de León and the Spanish Discovery of Puerto Rico and Florida* (Blacksburg, Va.: The MacDonald & Woodward Publishing Company, 2000), 51.
12. Douglas T. Peck, *Ponce de León and the Discovery of Florida: The Man, the Myth, and the Truth* (St. Paul, Minn.: Pogo Press, 1993), 9.
13. Fuson, *Juan Ponce de León and the Spanish Discovery of Puerto Rico and Florida*, 83.
14. Ibid., 88.
15. Fairbanks, *History of Florida*, 17.
16. Ibid.
17. Michael V. Gannon, *The Cross in the Sand: The Early Catholic Church in Florida, 1513–1870* (Gainesville: University Press of Florida, 1965, 1983), 2.
18. Ibid.
19. Ibid., 3.

Chapter 4

20. Ibid.
21. Ibid.
22. Mountjoy, *Francisco Coronado*, 19.
23. Ibid.
24. Ibid., 20.
25. Ibid., 22.
26. George P. Hammond, *Coronado's Seven Cities* (Albuquerque, N.M.: United States Coronado Exposition Commission, 1940), 1.
27. Gannon, *The Cross in the Sand*, 6.
28. Ibid.

29. Fuson, *Juan Ponce de León and the Spanish Discovery of Puerto Rico and Florida*, 191.

Chapter 5

30. Fairbanks, *The History and Antiquities of the City of St. Augustine, Florida*, 17.
31. Albert Manucy, *Sixteenth-Century St. Augustine: The People and Their Homes* (Gainesville: University Press of Florida, 1997), 9.
32. Fairbanks, *The History and Antiquities of the City of St. Augustine, Florida*, 17.
33. Ibid.
34. Ibid.
35. Ibid.
36. Ibid.
37. Eugene Lyon, *The Enterprise of Florida: Pedro Menéndez de Avilés and the Spanish Conquest of 1565–1568* (Gainesville: University Press of Florida, 1976), 53.
38. Ibid.

Chapter 6

39. Ibid., 71.
40. Ibid., 73.
41. Ibid., 71.
42. Ibid., 73.
43. Lyon, 72.
44. Manucy, *Sixteenth-Century St. Augustine: The People and Their Homes*, 9.
45. Amy Bushnell, *The Noble and Loyal City: 1565–1688*, as found in Jean Parker Waterbury, ed., *The Oldest City: St. Augustine, Saga of Survival* (St. Augustine, Fla.: The St. Augustine Historical Society, 1983), 29.

46. Lyon, *The Enterprise of Florida*, 115.
47. Ibid.
48. Fairbanks, *The History and Antiquities of the City of St. Augustine, Florida*, 19.
49. Ibid.
50. Michael V. Gannon, *Florida.* (Gainesville: University Press of Florida, 1993), 8.
51. Elaine Murray Stone, *Pedro Menéndez de Avilés and the Founding of St. Augustine* (New York: P.J. Kenedy & Sons, 1969), 59.
52. Ibid.

Chapter 7

53. Fairbanks, *History of Florida*, 118.
54. Ibid.
55. Ibid.
56. Ibid., 118–119.
57. Ibid., 119.
58. Lyon, *The Enterprise of Florida*, 121.
59. Ibid., 121–122.
60. Ibid., 122.
61. Fairbanks, *History of Florida*, 120.
62. Ibid.
63. Ibid.
64. Lyon, *The Enterprise of Florida*, 122.
65. Ibid., 123.
66. Fairbanks, *History of Florida*, 120.
67. Ibid.
68. Amy Bushnell, *The Noble and Loyal City*, 30.
69. Fairbanks, *History of Florida*, 125.

Chapter 8

70. Lyon, *The Enterprise of Florida*, 170.

Chapter 9

71. Fairbanks, *History of Florida*, 120.
72. Ibid., 150.
73. Ibid.
74. Albert Manucy, *Menéndez: Pedro Menéndez de Avilés, Captain General of the Ocean Sea* (Sarasota, Fla.: Pineapple Press, Inc., 1983), 91.
75. Ibid., 94.
76. George E. Buker, *The Americanization of St. Augustine: 1821–1865*, as found in Jean Parker Waterbury, ed., *The Oldest City: St. Augustine, Saga of Survival* (St. Augustine, Fla.: The San Augustine Historical Society, 1983), 151

Bibliography

Daegan, Kathleen A., ed. *America's Ancient City: Spanish St. Augustine 1565–1763*. New York & London: Garland Publishing, 1991.

Davenport, John C. *Juan Ponce de León and His Lands of Discovery*. Philadelphia: Chelsea House Publishers, 2005.

Fairbanks, George R. *The History and Antiquities of the City of St. Augustine, Florida* (reprint of the 1858 edition). Gainesville: University Press of Florida, 1975.

——. *History of Florida: From its Discovery by Ponce de León, in 1512, to the Close of the Florida War, in 1842*. Philadelphia: J.B. Lippincott & Co., 1871.

Fuson, Robert H. *Juan Ponce de León and the Spanish Discovery of Puerto Rico and Florida*. Blacksburg, Va.: The MacDonald & Woodward Publishing Company, 2000.

Gannon, Michael V. *The Cross in the Sand: The Early Catholic Church in Florida, 1513–1870*. Gainesville: University Press of Florida, 1965, 1983.

——. *Florida*. Gainesville: University Press of Florida, 1993.

Kapitzke, Robert L. *Religion, Power, and Politics in Colonial St. Augustine*. Gainesville: University Press of Florida, 2001.

Lyon, Eugene. *The Enterprise of Florida: Pedro Menéndez de Avilés and the Spanish Conquest of 1565–1568*. Gainesville: University Press of Florida, 1976.

Manucy, Albert. *Menéndez: Pedro Menéndez de Avilés, Captain General of the Ocean Sea*. Sarasota, Fla.: Pineapple Press, 1983.

——. *Sixteenth-Century St. Augustine: The People and Their Homes*. Gainesville: University Press of Florida, 1997.

McEwan, Bonnie G., ed. *The Spanish Mission of La Florida*. Gainesville: University Press of Florida, 1993.

Morrison, Samuel Eliot. *The European Discovery of America: The Southern Voyages, A.D. 1492–1616*. New York: Oxford University Press, 1974.

Mountjoy, Shane. *Francisco Coronado and the Seven Cities of Gold*. Philadelphia: Chelsea House Publishers, 2005.

——. *Francisco Pizarro and the Conquest of the Inca*. Philadelphia: Chelsea House Publishers, 2005.

Otfinoski, Steven. *Juan Ponce de León: Discoverer of Florida*. New York: Benchmark Books (Marshall Cavendish), 2005.

Peck, Douglas T. *Ponce de León and the Discovery of Florida: The Man, the Myth, and the Truth*. St. Paul, Minn.: Pogo Press, 1993.

Reitz, Elizabeth Jean. *Spanish and British Subsistence Strategies at St. Augustine, Florida and Frederica, Georgia, between 1565 and 1783*. Ann Arbor, Mich.: University Microfilms International, 1980.

Slavicek, Louise Chipley. *Juan Ponce de León*. Philadelphia: Chelsea House Publishers, 2003.

Stone, Elaine Murray. *Pedro Menéndez de Avilés and the Founding of St. Augustine*. New York: P.J. Kenedy & Sons, 1969.

Waterbury, Jean Parker, ed. *The Oldest City: St. Augustine: Saga of Survival*. St. Augustine, Fla.: The St. Augustine Historical Society, 1983.

Worth, Richard. *Ponce de León and the Age of Spanish Exploration in World History*. Berkeley Heights, N.J.: Enslow Publishers, 2003.

Further Reading

Barnes, Jay. *Florida's Hurricane History*. Chapel Hill, N.C.: University of North Carolina Press, 1998.

Brown, Robin C. *Florida's First People: 12,000 Years of Human History*. Sarasota, Fla.: Pineapple Press, 1994.

Burnett, Gene M. *Florida's Past: People and Events That Shaped the State*. Sarasota, Fla.: Pineapple Press, 1998.

Gannon, Michael. *The New History of Florida*. Gainesville, Fla.: University Press of Florida, 1996.

Harvey, Karen. *America's First City: St. Augustine's Historic Neighborhoods*. Lake Buena Vista, Fla.: Tailored Tours Publications, Inc., 1992.

Henderson, Ann L., and Gary R. Mormino. *Spanish Pathways in Florida: 1492–1992*. Sarasota, Fla.: Pineapple Press, 1991.

Milanich, Jerald T. *Florida's Indians From Ancient Time to the Present*. Gainesville, Fla.: University Press of Florida, 1998.

——. *Florida Indians and the Invasion from Europe*. Gainesville, Fla.: University Press of Florida, 1995.

Peirce, Neal R. *The Deep South States of America: People, Politics, and Power in the Seven Deep South States*. New York: W.W. Norton & Company, 1974.

Riehecky, Janet. *The Settling of St. Augustine*. Milwaukee, Wisc.: World Almanac Library, 2003.

Van Campen, J.T. *St. Augustine: Florida's Colonial Capital*. St. Augustine, Fla.: The St. Augustine Historical Society, 1959.

Web sites

A Brief History of Florida
http://www.flheritage.com/facts/history/summary/

St. Augustine: America's Ancient City
http://www.flmnh.ufl.edu/staugustine/intro.htm

The Founding of St. Augustine
http://www.fordham.edu/halsall/mod/1565staugustine.html

Castillo de San Marcos National Monument
http://www.nps.gov/casa

St. Augustine History and Information
http://www.oldcity.com/history-information.cfm

St. Augustine: History of the Nation's Oldest City
http://www.staugustinelinks.com/st-augustine-history.asp

Picture Credits

Index

About the Contributors

Series editor **TIM MCNEESE** is associate professor of history at York College in York, Nebraska, where he is in his fifteenth year of college instruction. Professor McNeese earned an Associate of Arts degree from York College, a Bachelor of Arts in history and political science from Harding University, and a Master of Arts in history from Missouri State University. A prolific author of books for elementary, middle and high school, and college readers, McNeese has published more than 80 books and educational materials over the past 20 years, on everything from Picasso to landmark Supreme Court decisions. His writing has earned him a citation in the library reference work *Contemporary Authors*. In 2006, he appeared on the History Channel program *Risk Takers/History Makers: John Wesley Powell and the Grand Canyon*.

Author **SHANE MOUNTJOY** lives in York, Nebraska, where he is associate professor of history at York College. Professor Mountjoy holds an Associate of Arts degree from York College, a Bachelor of Arts degree from Lubbock Christian University, a Master of Arts from the University of Nebraska-Lincoln, and a Doctor of Philosophy from the University of Missouri-Columbia. He and his wife, Vivian, home school their four daughters. A teacher and lover of history, geography, and political science, Dr. Mountjoy has written and edited more than 10 books.